Pat Collins

The Gifts of the Spirit
and the
New Evangelisation

the columba press

First published in 2009 by
the columba press
55A Spruce Avenue, Stillorgan Industrial Park,
Blackrock, Co Dublin

Cover by Bill Bolger
Origination by The Columba Press
Printed in Ireland by ColourBooks Ltd, Dublin

ISBN 978 1 85607 645 6

Table of Contents

ABBREVIATIONS USED

CCC	*Catechism of the Catholic Church*
CCL	*Code of Canon Law* (1983)
CD	*Christus Dominus* (Christ the Lord)
EE	*Ecclesia in Europa* (The Church in Europe)
EN	*Evangelii Nuntiandi* (On Evangelisation in the Modern World)
FEC	*(St Thomas's commentary) First Epistle to the Corinthians*
HV	*Heroic Virtue*
NMI	*Novo Millenio Inuente* (At the beginning of the New Millennium)
RM	*Redemptoris Missio* (Mission of the Redeemer)
SCG	*Summa Contra Gentiles* (Summary against the Gentiles)
SCP	*(St Thomas) Sermon and Collation of St Thomas Aquinas for the Feast of Pentecost*
ST	*Summa Theologica* (Summary of Theology)

Introduction

In the summer of 2005 I travelled to Detroit, Michigan to speak to Legatus, an organisation for Catholic business people. I stayed in Sacred Heart Major Seminary, in the centre of the city. While I was there I heard the rector of the college announce that an STL degree in the new evangelisation was going to be offered for the first time, in September 2006. He said that this Licentiate in Sacred Theology would be the only one of its kind in the world. Immediately, I thought that I'd love to do the degree because it was about evangelisation. Well, to cut a longer story short, having got permission from my Vincentian superior, I applied to the college and was accepted. With the support of parishioners in St Valentine's Parish, Redford, and a lot of hard work, I graduated in the summer of 2008.

While in Detroit I gave good deal of thought to the role of the gifts of the Holy Spirit in the new evangelisation and decided to write this book about the subject. It seeks, in some small way, to respond to the challenge of Pope Paul VI in par. 75 of *Evangelii Nuntiandii*, where he expressed the desire that 'pastors and theologians ... should study more thoroughly the nature and manner of the Holy Spirit's action in evangelisation today.' This study, as you will see, contains many references to authoritative writings, such as the scriptures, Fathers of the Church, Popes, St Thomas Aquinas, etc. There are also numerous footnotes and a lengthy bibliography which are intended, not only to inform, but also to act as a resource for those who are interested in pursuing the subject at a deeper level. My hope is that this short venture into pastoral theology will prove to be a useful contribution to those who wish to engage in effective evangelisation.

A PROPHETIC CONTEXT

At this point I'd like to put the new evangelisation in context. I am aware that this brief section is a rather subjective interpretation of the signs of the times. Nevertheless, I thought I'd include it because I have long believed that scripture is correct when it says, 'Without prophecy the people become demoralised' Prov 29:18. Over the years I have heard many prophecies which have been uttered in Christian circles. It is notoriously hard to know whether they come from God or not. However, there are some which have considerable authority because of the circumstances in which they were spoken, the acknowledged giftedness of the people who spoke them, and the way in which they evoked an answering amen of approval in the Christian community. On Pentecost Monday 1975 such a prophecy was given by Ralph Martin in St Peter's Basilica, Rome, in the presence of Pope Paul VI. Ever since, it has been referred to in Catholic circles. It seems to contain a number of distinct but interrelated points.

a) A time of darkness and purification in the church

Firstly, the Lord seemed to predict that a time of purifying darkness was about to afflict the church. 'Open your eyes, open your hearts to prepare yourselves for me and for the day that I have now begun. My church will be different; my people will be different; difficulties and trials will come upon you ... I will lead you into the desert ... I will strip you of everything that you are depending on now, so you depend just on me.'[1] The Lord went on to say more about the purpose of the time of trial and purification. 'You need the power of my Holy Spirit in a way that you have not possessed it; you need an understanding of my will and of the ways I work that you do not yet have.' Thirty-three years later, would it not be true to say that this aspect of the prophecy has been fulfilled. The church has been afflicted ever since it was first spoken. It is as if the powers of hell have been unleashed, in order to mount an attack on the people of God. One is reminded in this context of words spoken by Jesus, 'behold, Satan demanded to have you, that he might sift you like

---

1. http://www.renewalministries.net/pdfs/Prophecies_Pentecost_ Monday.pdf (accessed Oct 6th 2008).

wheat' (Lk 22:31). When he was in Ireland in 1979, Pope John Paul echoed that point in a prophetic way at Limerick, 'Your country ... is being asked to prefer the kingdoms of this world with their splendour to the kingdom of God (Mt 4:8). Satan, the tempter, the adversary of Christ will use all his might and deceptions to win Ireland for the way of the world ... Now is the time of testing for Ireland. This generation is once more a generation of decision.'

The effects of this time of trial are fairly obvious. Many people have failed in the day of testing. For instance, in places such as Europe, the USA, and Australia practice rates, together with vocations to the priesthood and religious life have fallen rapidly. It is hard to establish exact figures. When interviewed, respondents often exaggerate the frequency of their weekly Mass attendance. In Italy, for example, about one third of the population claim to attend weekly Mass, but empirical research suggests that *de facto* about 16% do so. The figure is around 18% in Spain and 12% in France. The figures for Austria, Germany and the Netherlands are between 10-15%.[2] There is good reason to believe that in the period between 1984 and 2004 the numbers attending weekly Mass in Ireland fell by half, from over 80% to just over 40%. So by international standards, the figures are still relatively high. But will they continue to fall, as they have done in Quebec, from about 88% to around 23%?[3] As far as vocations are concerned, they are about one-tenth of what they were forty years ago. For instance, in 2004 only 15 men were ordained in Ireland. There also has been a decline in Christian morality. This is particularly obvious where sexuality is concerned. More and more couples live together outside of marriage; most married and unmarried partners use artificial forms of contraception; the incidence of births to single mothers is rising; a growing number of men are get involved with pornography especially on the internet; and many people advocate abortion as a solution to un-

2. The European statistics are taken from Philip Jenkins's *God's Continent: Christianity, Islam, and Europe's Religious Crisis* (Oxford: Oxford University Press, 2007), 30.
3. *The Church Confronts Modernity: Catholicism Since 1950 in the United States, Ireland, and Quebec,* ed. Leslie Woodcock Tentler (Washington: Catholic University of America Press, 2007), 6.

wanted pregnancy. Added to this there are other indications of declining morals such as a rising level of violence, binge drinking, drug taking and dishonesty. Is it any wonder that John Paul II observed, 'European culture gives the impression of "silent apostasy" on the part of people who have all that they need and who live as if God does not exist.'[4]

Secondly, while all of this was happening there was also a growing minority of Christian men and women who not only remained faithful during the years of darkness, many of them grew in age, wisdom, and grace. For example, they have rejected the reductionist, anti-supernatural bias of a good deal of liberal theology in order to adhere to the magisterium of the church which not only believes in God, but also in the divinity of Jesus, the bodily resurrection of the dead, the existence of good and evil spirits, and the possibility of such things as healing, miracles and exorcism. Nowadays there is a significant number of praying people who are firmly committed to Christ and his teaching and who try conscientiously to answer the universal calls to holiness and evangelisation.

b) A time of darkness in the secular world
The prophecy given in St Peter's in 1975 seemed to say that the time of darkness in the church would be followed by a time of darkness in the secular world. 'Days of darkness are coming on the world, days of tribulation.' I have believed for many years that a time was coming when there would be great disruption and even breakdown in the secular world. Indeed I can remember saying just that in a book I published in 1995. For instance at one point I wrote, 'Bernard Lonergan … described in a cogent and disturbing way, how whole societies can experience decline as a result of such things as selfishness, subjectivism and a lack of transcendental awareness.[5] When values and beliefs get "corrupted" to use Lonergan's word, they are disseminated by the mass media, the education system and the prevailing philosophies of the time. 'A civilisation in decline,' he concluded, 'digs its own grave with relentless consistency. It cannot be argued

---

4. *Ecclesia in Europa*, par., 9
5. 'Progress and Decline' *Method in Theology* (London: Darton, Longman & Todd), 52-53.

out of its destructive way.' In the coming years it is possible that, as a result of growing irrationality and moral blindness, we may have to endure a time of economic and political disruption … No matter how painful the dislocation of society may be, it could lead many people to reject questionable philosophical and economic beliefs, just as it has already done in the former Soviet Union.'[6] However the breakdown might occur, it would have two predictable effects. It would cause some people to say, 'let us eat, drink and be merry for tomorrow we die!' (cf. Eccl 8:15) and others to say, 'let us seek the Lord while he may still be found' (Is 55:6). St Paul observed, 'Godly sorrow brings repentance that leads to salvation and leaves no regret, but worldly sorrow brings death' (2 Cor 7:10-11). At the time of writing, October 2008, it looks as if the predicted time of secular darkness is already beginning in the form of collapsing financial institutions, falling share prices and the likelihood of a world wide recession or even depression.

c) A new springtime for the church

This brings us to a third point in the prophecy. The Lord intends to use his committed followers, whom he raised up and equipped during the church's time of darkness, to evangelise those who will seek him during the time of darkness in the secular world. As the Lord said in the prophecy in St Peter's, 'A time of darkness is coming on the world, but a time of glory is coming for my church, a time of glory is coming for my people … I will prepare you for a time of evangelism that the world has not seen.' The great English Pentecostal, Smith Wigglesworth, uttered a similar prophecy in 1947 shortly before he died. He predicted the rise of the Charismatic Movement and the House Church Movement. Then he went on to predict that both of them would decline. Then he said, 'When the new church phase is on the wane, there will be evidence in the churches of something that has not been seen before: a coming together of those with an emphasis on the word and those with an emphasis on the Spirit. When the word and the Spirit come together, there will be the

---

6. *Unveiling the Heart: How to Overcome Evil in the Christian Life*, (Dublin: Veritas, 1995), 49.

biggest move of the Holy Spirit that the nation, and indeed, the world has ever seen. It will mark the beginning of a revival that will eclipse anything that has been witnessed within these shores, even the Wesleyan and Welsh revivals of former years. The outpouring of God's Spirit ... will begin a missionary move to the ends of the earth.' The first two of Wigglesworth's predictions have already been fulfilled. His notion of revival seems analogous to John Paul's talk about a springtime to come. Like the Roman prophecy in 1975, he spoke about a great age of evangelisation which would follow a new outpouring of the Holy Spirit.

I was interested to see that Ralph Martin, who spoke the prophecy in St Peter's in 1975, said in the year 1999 that he had reason to believe that the fulfilment of this word might be imminent. He wrote: 'I believe that we are now in a time of visitation. God is visiting us in the ministry of the Pope (John Paul II), in the ministry of Mary (in different apparitions where she warned people) and in many other ways as well. The time of preparation is well advanced. According to the message of John Paul and Mary *we are on the verge of a significant action of God* [my italics], an action that will function as a two edged sword, depending on our preparation and willingness to respond to the prophetic message we are being given. And is it not possible that the fullness of the 'new springtime' will not come until we are first purified through judgement or chastisement, and awakened to the holiness of God.'[7] It is not clear from what he says whether Martin is talking about the judgement and chastisement that is afflicting the church, or is about to afflict the world. Arguably, it is both.[8] One way or the other, the Lord will bring in the new springtime by means of widespread evangelisation which will only occur when a sufficient number of people has responded positively to the time of testing and purification.

As the third millennium approached, John Paul II spoke increasingly about a new springtime in the church. For example, in *Redemptoris Missio* par. 86 he wrote: 'As the third millennium of the redemption draws near, God is preparing a great spring-

---

7. 'New Springtime or Chastisement?' *Goodnews* (May/June 1999), 1-3.
8. Cf. Pat Collins CM, "Two Disasters one Call to Repentance,' *Spirituality* (July/August 2005), 224-229.

time for Christianity, and we can already see its first signs. In fact both in the non-Christian world and in the traditionally Christian world, people are gradually drawing closer to gospel ideals and values, a development which the Church seeks to encourage.'[9] From a biblical point of view, the new springtime has a paradoxical dimension. The Jews planted their seeds in the autumn when the early rains fell. They harvested the crops in the springtime following the later rain (cf Deut 11:14-15; Joel 2:23-24; Jas 5:7). Some writers say that reference to the early and late rains can be applied in a symbolic way to an initial outpouring of the Holy Spirit, e.g. at the birth of the Pentecostal and Charismatic Movements, and hopefully a later outpouring of the Spirit in the not too distant future, as a preparation for the harvesting of a great number of souls for God.

A TIME OF REBUILDING

The predicted springtime will be ushered in by the new evangelisation. One way of preparing is to continue to rebuild the breaches in the spiritual walls of the church. In Neh 2:20, the prophet says: 'The God of heaven is the one who will give us success, and we his servants are going to start building.' In Hag 1:8-9 we read, 'Go up to the hills and bring wood and build the house, that I may take pleasure in it and that I may appear in my glory, says the Lord. You have looked for much, and, lo, it came to little; and when you brought it home, I blew it away. Why? says the Lord of hosts. Because of my house that lies in ruins, while you busy yourselves each with his own house.' A little later in verse fourteen we read that, 'the remnant of the people came and worked on the house of the Lord of hosts, their God.' Many centuries later St Francis engaged in prophetic action of a similar, symbolic kind, when, with the help of friends, he set himself to repair five churches in Assisi. He did this because he heard the Lord say, 'Francis, go and build up my house, as you see, is falling into ruin.'[10] When the work was completed we are

---

9. Cf Eduardo J Echeverria Ph.D, 'A Great Springtime for Christianity,' *John Paul II and the New Evangelization*, ed. Ralph Martin & Peter Williamson (Cincinnati: Servant Books, 2006), 288-295.

told that, 'he began to preach the gospel'[11] in order to rebuild the walls of Christ's spiritual church. In the next few years a great deal of restoration will be required in the lives of the people of God so that it will be readied to engage, not only in the new evangelisation mentioned in the prophecy given in St Peter's in 1975, but also in receiving into the Christian community those who will want to joyfully commit their lives to Christ.

PURPOSE OF THE BOOK

This book seeks to indicate that not only are there reasonable exegetical and theological grounds for classifying the gifts of the Spirit in 1 Cor 12:8-10 as gifts of revelation, proclamation, and demonstration, it seeks to show why they have an important role to play in the new evangelisation called for by the church. This contention will not only be supported by examining the gospels, and Paul's first letter to the Corinthians, but also by studying relevant sections in a number of the writings of St Thomas Aquinas and Benedict XIV. It will conclude with an examination of contemporary writing on the connection between so called 'baptism in the Spirit' and evangelisation in Christian scholarship.

The book will seek to indicate that the gifts of the Spirit which have been restored by the providence of God in recent years, can reveal the numinous presence and power of the Lord to a generation that is losing faith in the supernatural dimension of life. As Pope Paul VI said on one occasion: 'At the same time, the breath-giving influence of the Spirit has come to awaken latent forces within the church, to stir up forgotten charisms and to infuse that sense of vitality and joy which in every epoch of history marks the church itself as youthful and up-to-date, ready and happy again to proclaim its eternal message to the modern age.'[12] Like the Baptist of old the charisms prepare the way for the Lord by opening minds and hearts to the transform-

---

10. St Bonaventure, *The Life of St Francis of Assisi* (Rockford, Ill.: Tan Books, 1988), 18.
11. Ibid., 25.
12. Edward D. O'Connor CSC, *Pope Paul and the Holy Spirit: Charisms and Church Renewal in the Teaching of Paul VI* (Notre Dame: Ave Maria Press, 1978), 201.

ing power of the kerygmatic proclamation of the evangelisers.

ACKNOWLEDGEMENTS

There are many people I want to thank. Firstly, there are my Vincentian colleagues who enabled me to study evangelisation. They also supported a desire to explore new ways of spreading the good news and training would-be evangelisers. Secondly, I owe a great debt of gratitude to the staff of Sacred Heart Major Seminary in Detroit, and to my fellow students who did so much to increase my zeal for evangelisation. While in the motor city, the priests, parish staff and parishioners in St Val's offered me warm hospitality, friendship and on-going encouragement. Thirdly, I offer heartfelt gratitude to the many friends I have made in the Charismatic Movement, especially in Ireland, Britain and Italy over the last 34 years. I also greatly admire the many wonderful men and women who work for Alpha Ireland. They never cease to impress and inspire me by their goodness and heartfelt desire to make Jesus known and loved by as many people as possible. Lastly, I know that there are many highly motivated Catholics and Protestants who are just waiting to be mobilised in the great cause of evangelisation. Over the years, many of them have told me about their readiness to answer this call. Please God, the time has come to summon them to the great task of rebuilding the breached walls of the Christian community, so that it may once again be a like a city built on a hill whose glory and light cannot be hidden (cf Mt 5:14). There is so much to do. It is time to begin.

CHAPTER ONE

What is The New Evangelisation?

It is my belief that a revolutionary change is currently taking place in the Catholic Church, one that many clergy and lay people do not yet fully appreciate. As Cardinal Avery Dulles SJ has pointed out in an article entitled, 'John Paul II and the New Evangelization: What Does it Mean?'[1] it is a striking fact that although the words evangelise and evangelisation[2] were not even mentioned at Vatican I, they were referred to no fewer than 31 times at Vatican II. Ever since then the Popes, especially Paul VI and John Paul II, have repeatedly stressed the need for Catholics to engage in evangelisation. In par. 14 of his apostolic exhortation, *Evangelii Nuntiandi* (hereafter *EN*), Paul VI wrote: 'We wish to confirm once more that the task of evangelising all people constitutes the essential mission of the church. It is a task and mission which the vast and profound changes of present-day society make all the more urgent. Evangelising is in fact the grace and vocation proper to the church, *her deepest identity. She exists to evangelise* (my italics).'

Some time later, John Paul II said in his encyclical letter *Redemptoris Missio* (hereafter *RM*) par. 3, 'I sense that the moment has come to commit all of the church's energies to the new evangelisation.' It is worth noting that the Holy Father didn't say that the church should devote some, or many of its resources to a new evangelisation, but rather, *all* of them. In the same paragraph he added, '*No believer in Christ, no institution of the church* [my italics] can avoid this supreme duty: to proclaim Christ to all peoples.' Some years later, not long before his death, the Holy Father eloquently said in par. 40 of *Novo Millenio Inuente* (hereafter *NMI*), 'Over the years, I have often repeated the summons to the new evangelisation. I do so again now, especially in order to insist that we must rekindle in ourselves the impetus of the

---

1. *John Paul II and the New Evangelization*, ed. Ralph Martin & Peter Williamson (Cincinnati: Servant Books, 2006), 2-16
2. (San Francisco: Harper and Row, 1980), 214.

beginnings and allow ourselves to be filled with the ardour of the apostolic preaching which followed Pentecost. We must revive in ourselves the burning conviction of Paul, who cried out: "Woe to me if I do not preach the gospel" (1 Cor 9:16).'

WHAT IS EVANGELISATION?

In the New Testament sense, the verb 'evangelise' means to proclaim with authority and power the good news of salvation in Jesus Christ. The word comes from God and arouses saving faith. So to evangelise is to announce, in accordance with the faith of the church, the good news of God's saving work in Jesus Christ. It does this with a view to bringing the hearer/s to personal faith in the Lord and a life of committed discipleship. In *EN* par. 18, Pope Paul offered a definition of evangelisation, while pointing out that it actually has two sides, personal and collective. To paraphrase his words, evangelising means bringing the good news of Jesus into every human situation and seeking to convert individuals and society by the divine power of the gospel message itself. In *EN* par. 27, the pontiff said: 'Evangelisation will always contain – as the foundation, centre, and at the same time, summit of its dynamism – a clear proclamation that, in Jesus Christ, the Son of God made man, who died and rose from the dead, salvation is offered to all men, as a gift of God's grace and mercy.' That word salvation is crucial. It raises the question, saved from what? In Christian terms we are saved from sin, Satan, and the eternal loss of God. This raises a problem. Many people today have lost an objective sense of sin. While the Bible says, 'I have done what is evil *in your sight* (my italics)' (Ps 51:4), nowadays many of our contemporaries are inclined to say in a subjective way, 'I have rarely if ever done what is evil *in my sight*.' I know as a confessor that numerous men and women tend to avoid personal responsibility for wrongdoing by explaining away their actions and omissions in terms of personal needs, and pressures of an unconscious or a social kind. Many of them neither believe in the existence of Satan the tempter, the father of lies, the murderer (cf Jn 8:44), or of hell as an eternal state of miserable separation from God. They stress the love of God in a way that implies that the Lord overlooks bad behaviour in a permissive manner, while studiously ignoring any mention of the biblical notions of God's justice, anger or punishments. If these topics are referred to they will say such things as, 'Don't tell me you are reviving the fire and brimstone version of Christianity!' or 'Your approach sounds very negative, fearful and judgemental. I thought we had moved beyond that sort of thing.' As a result it is difficult for them to acknowledge their need for divine salvation.

The American bishops said in par. 23 of *Go and Make Disciples* (1992) that evangelisation has an inward and an outward orientation. Inwardly it calls for our continued reception of the gospel of Jesus Christ, and ongoing conversion both as individuals and as church. It nurtures people, making them grow, and renews them in holiness as God's people. Outwardly evangelisation addresses those who have not yet heard the gospel or who, having heard it, have stopped practising their faith, and those who seek the fullness of faith. In *RM* par. 33, Pope John Paul II, summed up the three objectives of evangelisation: to proclaim the gospel to all people; to help bring about the re-conversion of those who have received the gospel but live it only nominally; and to deepen the gospel in the lives of believers.

Anyone who reads what the church has to say about evangelisation will quickly come to appreciate the fact that the word is used to describe many interrelated but different activities. Here are some of them.

1. Pre-evangelisation (cf *EN* par. 51) i.e. preparing the ground, usually by means of such things as living among those who may be evangelised in the future by Christian witness, social analysis and learning the language. All this is done with a view to the explicit proclamation of the gospel when the people are ready to receive it. However, the initial activities are already an intimation of full evangelisation and inseparable from it.

2. Primary evangelisation i.e. the early stages of evangelisation by means of proclamation and witness which aim to get the church properly established. Arguably there are four sequential steps involved in this process.

a) *Proclamation* of the kingdom by means of inspired preaching. Announcing God's reign, through the outpouring of un-conditional and unrestricted mercy and love, particularly upon those who are materially or spiritually poor.

b) *Demonstration* of the coming of the kingdom, either through deeds of merciful love or deeds of power such as healing and exorcism.

c) *Repentance.* In the light of the proclamation/demonstration of the kingdom, the evangelist invites people to turn away from their sin in order to accept Jesus and his way of living, in faith.

d) *Discipleship.* Telling those who have accepted Christ how they can become his disciples by willingly accepting to carry the yoke of the Christian ethic as the expression of heartfelt commitment to him.

3. Secondary-evangelisation i.e. helping sacramentalised Christians who have received the sacraments of initiation to commit, or re-commit themselves, to the good news in nominally Christian communities/societies. Speaking about the distinction between primary and secondary evangelisation *RM* par. 37 says: 'It seems wrong to make no distinction between a people that has never known Christ and a people that has known him and rejected him, but continues to live in a culture permeated to a large extent by gospel principles. As far as the faith is concerned these two situations are quite different.' Arguably it is easier to convert a person who is a non-Christian in Africa than a disillusioned ex-Catholic in Europe or America.

4. Catechesis i.e. literally echoing the Christian teaching, building on the basics by means of planned, systematic teaching, in order to bring about 'a living, explicit and active faith enlightened by instruction.'[3] It builds upon the foundation stone of discipleship which is laid by means of primary evangelisation.

5. Action for justice. There is a growing realisation in the contemporary church that there is no true evangelisation without action for justice. The 1971 Synod of Bishops said in *Justice in the World* that the social ministries of the church are an essential part of its preaching mission, 'Activity on behalf of justice is a constitutive part of preaching the gospel.'[4] As a

---

3. *Christus Dominus* par. 14.

4. *Justice in the World* (Washington: United States Catholic Conference, 1971), 34.

result Christians have to alleviate poverty and also identify and remove its causes in the sinful and oppressive structures of society.

When the subject of evangelisation is discussed in Christian circles, misunderstandings often arise because people fail to appreciate the fact that the word has many interrelated meanings. This book will focus mainly on points two and three, namely, primary and secondary evangelisation.

THE CONTENT OF PRIMARY AND SECONDARY EVANGELISATION

As par. 11 of the *Decree on Ecumenism* points out, in Christianity there is a hierarchy of truths. We refer to the foundational truths of faith as the *kerygma* (in Greek it means, proclamation, announcement, preaching). C. H. Dodd suggested in the first chapter of his influential book, *The Apostolic Preaching and Its Developments*,[5] that the kerygma has six key elements.

1. The Age of Fulfillment has dawned, the 'latter days' foretold by the prophets.
2. This has taken place through the birth, life, ministry, death and resurrection of Jesus Christ
3. By virtue of the resurrection, Jesus has been exalted at the right hand of God as messianic head of the new Israel.
4. The Holy Spirit in the church is the sign of Christ's present power and glory.
5. The messianic age will reach its consummation in the return of Christ.
6. An appeal is made for repentance with the offer of forgiveness, the Holy Spirit, and salvation.

There are a number of kerygmatic statements in the New Testament.[6] For example, if you wanted to see a very brief version you could look at Acts 16:30-31. The jailer at Philippi was about to commit suicide when he cried out to Paul and Silas, 'Sirs, what must I do to be saved?' When they replied, 'Believe in the Lord Jesus, and you will be saved – you and your household' they were summarising the kerygma. There is a slightly longer

---

5. (San Francisco: Harper and Row, 1964).
6. Cf Raniero Cantalamessa's description of the kerygma in *The Holy Spirit in the Life of Jesus* (Collegeville: The Liturgical Press, 1994), 42-50.

version in Acts 8:36-38 where we are told that when Philip and the Ethiopian official went along the road they came to some water, and the eunuch said, 'See, here is water! What is to prevent my being baptised?' In some Western manuscripts, Philip is said to have replied, 'If you believe with all your heart, you may. And he said in reply, I believe that Jesus Christ is the Son of God.' St Peter preached an expanded version of the kerygma in Acts 4:8-12 when he proclaimed in the power of the Spirit: 'Rulers of the people and elders, if we are being examined today concerning a good deed done to a cripple, by what means this man has been healed, be it known to you all, and to all the people of Israel, that by the name of Jesus Christ of Nazareth, whom you crucified, whom God raised from the dead, by him this man is standing before you well. This is the stone which was rejected by you builders, but which has become the head of the corner. And there is salvation in no one else, for there is no other name under heaven given among men by which we must be saved.'

The challenge for those engaged in the new evangelisation is to express those primary truths in a way that makes sense in contemporary culture. In 1999 a joint declaration on justification was published by the Lutheran World Federation and the Catholic Church. Par. 15 says: 'Together we confess: By grace alone, in faith in Christ's saving work and not because of any merit on our part, we are accepted by God and receive the Holy Spirit, who renews our hearts while equipping and calling us to good works.'[7] Not only is this statement very significant from an ecumenical point of view, it encapsulates a key aspect of the good news. When that glorious truth falls from head to heart, it brings a person into a deep, joy-filled, personal faith in Christ and his saving work. Once people are established in the liberating experience of salvation, it can be built upon by means of catechesis i.e. a systematic instruction in the Christian faith.

We sometimes make two mistakes, however, in contemporary Christianity. Firstly, we tend to presume that, because people are baptised and confirmed, they are already aware of the power of the kerygma. As a result, most of the teaching that is given in church and in school attempts to build on the sand of

7. The document has since been endorsed by the Methodist Church.

this questionable assumption. Secondly, because we mistakenly believe that sacramentalised Christians are also evangelised, we expect them to carry the yoke of Christian ethics e.g. to do with such things as avoiding artificial contraception, divorce, pre-marital sex, and abortion. While many un-evangelised Christians may have the desire to carry the yoke of Christian ethics, they will not have the power to do so, because that power only comes when the kerygma is experienced in a personal way. As a result, many Christians live lives of ethical defeat, disillusionment and condemnation. Consequently they associate Christianity with bad rather than good news.[8] Recognising these twin problems, the new evangelisation concentrates, first and foremost, on pro-claiming the basic Christian truths e.g. by means of such things as Alpha courses and Life in the Spirit seminars.

WHAT IS THE NEW EVANGELISATION?

The late Pope John Paul II explained that this evangelisation is not new in content, 'The new evangelisation,' he said, 'begins with the clear and emphatic proclamation of the gospel ... it must in no way compromise the distinctiveness and integrity of the Christian faith.' In 1991, while commissioning families of the Neo-Catechumenal Way the Holy Father stated: 'The task which awaits you – the new evangelisation – demands that you present ... *the eternal and unchanging content of the heritage of the Christian faith* [my italics]. As you well know it is not a matter of merely passing on a doctrine, but rather of a personal and profound meeting with the Saviour.' Speaking to the American Church, the pontiff said: 'The vital core of the new evangelisation must be a clear and unequivocal proclamation of the person of Jesus Christ.'[9] In a talk given in 2000, Cardinal Joseph Ratzinger, now Pope Benedict XVI, went on to explain to catechists in Rome that the new evangelisation focuses on four key topics, conversion, the kingdom of God, Jesus Christ and eternal life.[10]

---

8. There are similarities between this experience and what St Paul re-ferred to as living a life of servitude under the law (cf Rom 4:15; 5:20; 7:9; 2 Cor 3:6; Gal 3:19).
9. *The Church in America*, par. 66.
10. Address to a world gathering of catechists and religion teachers in Rome, December 10, 2000.

Although the gospel is unchanging, the culture in which it is proclaimed is changing all the time, so the good news has to be inculturated, i.e. expressed in a contemporary way that will make sense to the people of our time. In *RM* par. 52, Pope John Paul II said that inculturation, 'means the intimate transformation of authentic cultural values, through their integration in Christianity and the insertion of Christianity in the various human cultures.' In pars. 58-60 of *Ecclesia in Europa* (hereafter *EE*) he spelt out the implications for our respective countries. To do this effectively, John Paul explained in a much quoted phrase, a proclamation is needed that is new in 'ardour, methods and forms of expression.'

I think it would be true to say that there are two main forms of evangelisation. On the one hand there are the traditional foreign missions which seek to bring the good news to non-Christians in foreign countries e.g. in Africa or Asia, and on the other hand there is the new evangelisation which seeks to evangelise or re-evangelise people who live in traditionally Christian cultures like Ireland and Britain. The new evangelisation is the home mission, so to speak.

WHO IS THE FOCUS OF THE NEW EVANGELISATION?

The new evangelisation focuses on the following groups.

Firstly, as was noted already, there are practising Catholics who are sacramentalised but not fully evangelised.[11] As we know, there are many people who, in spite of attending church on a regular basis, do not seem to have either a personal relationship with Christ or a firm inner conviction that they are justified, not by their personal merit, but by grace through their faith in Christ's saving death and resurrection (cf Gal 2:16). Often the creedal faith that church goers profess on Sunday fails to have a discernible impact on the way in which they live during the week, e.g. in matters of business and sexual ethics. I have noticed in recent years that some Christians adopt a liberal, reductionist version of religion. They doubt such things as the physical resur-

---

11. Pope Paul VI was quite right when he said in *EN* par. 47, 'In a certain sense it is a mistake to make a contrast between evangelisation and sacramentalisation, as is sometimes done.'

rection of Jesus, the existence of good or bad angels, the legitimacy of petitionary prayer, the possibility of healing, miracles or exorcism or receiving revelation from God. There are others who adopt a syncretistic approach by trying to synthesise Christian and non-Christian beliefs, e.g. those associated with the New Age.[12] Presumably, Paul VI had something like this in mind when he wrote in *EN* par. 15, 'The church is an evangeliser, but she begins by being evangelised herself ... She needs to listen unceasingly to what she must believe, to her reasons for hoping, to the new commandment of love.'

Nowadays, there is a good deal of talk about the unchurched, i.e. lapsed people who are inactive for a long time and who only turn up in church for baptisms, deaths and marriages. Speaking about them, Paul VI said in *EN* par. 56, 'There are a great numbers of people who have been baptised and, while they have not formally renounced their membership of the church, are as it were on the fringe of it and do not live according to her teaching.' In *EN* par. 56, Pope Paul explained with his characteristic insightfulness that people lapse as a result of such things as, 'natural weakness, a profound inconsistency which we unfortunately bear deep within us. Today however it shows certain new characteristics. It is often the result of the uprooting typical of our time. It also springs from the fact that Christians live in close proximity with non-believers and constantly experience the effects of unbelief. Furthermore, the non-practising Christians of today, more so than those of previous periods, seek to explain and justify their position in the name of an interior religion, of personal independence or authenticity.'

Finally there are unbelievers such as agnostics and atheists as well as members of other faiths such as Jews, Moslems, and Hindus. We are called to evangelise them also. Cardinal Ratzinger, now Pope Benedict XVI, warned in *Dominus Jesus*, that Catholics should avoid a false form of political correctness which maintains that all religions are equally valid ways to God. In spite of the fact that non-Christian religions can be means of

---

12. Cf Pontifical Council for Culture & Pontifical Council for Inter religious Dialogue, *Jesus Christ the Bearer of the Water of Life: A Christian reflection on the 'New Age'.*

grace, as par. 16 of the *Dogmatic Constitution on the Church* makes clear, we need to be convinced that what Paul said in 1 Tim 2:5 is crucially important: 'There is one God and one mediator between God and men, the man Jesus Christ.'

It is worth noting that canon 771 of the 1983 *Code of Canon Law* (hereafter *CCL*) says in part one, 'Pastors of souls, especially bishops and pastors, are to be concerned that the word of God is also proclaimed to those of the faithful who because of the condition of their life do not have sufficient common and ordinary pastoral care or lack it completely.' This part of the canon is referring to people such as migrants, exiles and refugees, seafarers, air-travellers, gypsies, and others of this kind. In all likelihood it also refers to the un-churched in a parish. It is not uncommon in Western countries to find that they constitute about two thirds of those who were baptised and confirmed. Part two of the canon goes on to say, 'They [i.e. the bishops and pastors etc.] are also to make provision that the message of the gospel reaches non-believers living in the territory since the care of souls must also extend to them no less than to the faithful.' This can be done by such things as the media, inter-religious dialogue and the witness of unconditional love. Would it not be true to say that there is a widespread failure to implement this canon?

MOTIVES FOR EVANGELISING

First and foremost there is the great commission of Jesus in Mk 16:15. We proclaim the coming of the kingdom of God as Jesus told us to do. As Pope John Paul II said in par. 18 of *RM*, 'The kingdom of God is not a concept, a doctrine, or a programme subject to free interpretation, but it is before all else a person with the face and name of Jesus of Nazareth, the image of the invisible God.' Pope Paul VI said in *EN* par. 24, 'The person who has been evangelised goes on to evangelise others. Here lies the test of truth, the touchstone of evangelisation: it is unthinkable that a person should accept the Word and give himself to the kingdom without becoming a person who bears witness to it and proclaims it in his turn.'

Secondly, we evangelists see the world *sub specie aeternatitis*, i.e. with the next world in mind. As Paul VI said in *EN* par. 28

'Evangelisation cannot but include the prophetic proclamation of a hereafter.' Unlike the false shepherds of Israel in Ezek 34:1-10, we try to share in the ardent zeal of Jesus, the good shepherd, who said in the parable of the lost sheep, 'Suppose one of you has a hundred sheep and loses one of them. Does he not leave the ninety-nine in the open country and go after the lost sheep until he finds it?' (Lk 15:3-4). Many liberal Christians believe that there are very few lost sheep because they assume that the road to heaven is wide and that many take it. As was noted earlier, they stress the love of God while overlooking divine justice. However, that is not what Jesus taught. In Mt 7:13-14 he said: 'Enter through the narrow gate. For wide is the gate and broad is the road that leads to destruction, and many enter through it. But small is the gate and narrow the road that leads to life, and only a few find it.'

St Paul echoed that disturbing point on a number of occasions. In Gal 5:19-21 he wrote, 'The acts of the sinful nature are obvious: sexual immorality, impurity and debauchery; idolatry and witchcraft; hatred, discord, jealousy, fits of rage, selfish ambition, dissensions, factions and envy; drunkenness, orgies, and the like. I warn you, as I did before, that those who live like this will not inherit the kingdom of God.' In Eph 5:5-6 he said something similar: 'You can be quite certain that nobody who actually indulges in fornication or impurity or promiscuity, which is worshipping a false god, can inherit anything of the kingdom of God. Do not let anyone deceive you with empty arguments: it is for this loose living that God's anger comes down on those who rebel against him.' Those who engage in the new evangelisation are animated by a heartfelt desire not only to reveal the dangers of sinful living, but more importantly to reveal the unconditional mercy and love of God in such an anointed way that it invites people to admit, and confess their sins, while opening their hearts to God's liberating self-communication in the Holy Spirit. Francis of Assisi was wont to say that nothing was to be preferred to the salvation of souls.[13] As the Lord says in Ezek 33:9: 'If you (the evangelist) warn the wicked to turn from his way,

---

13. St Bonaventure, *The Life of St Francis of Assisi* (Rockford, Ill.: Tan Books, 1988), 88.

and he does not turn from his way; he shall die in his iniquity, but you will have saved your life.'

Thirdly, over the last twenty years we have witnessed the decline of Christian practice. I am utterly convinced that if we are generous in sharing our faith with others it may halt and reverse the decline because our own faith will be deepened and strengthened in the process. As Jesus said to the disciples in Lk 6:38, 'Give, and it will be given to you. A good measure, pressed down, shaken together and running over, will be poured into your lap. For with the measure you use, it will be measured to you.' Pope John Paul II had that truth in mind when he said in *RM* par. 2, 'Faith is strengthened when it is given to others!' Again in *RM* par. 81 we read, 'Generosity in giving must always be enlightened and inspired by faith: then we will truly be more blessed in giving than receiving.' Finally in *RM* par. 85, John Paul said, 'It is by giving generously of what we have that we will receive.'

HOW TO EVANGELISE

This is a huge subject. I will only make seven brief, overlapping suggestions here. Firstly, echoing a point already made, we need to share in Christ's heart for the lost. His attitude is well expressed in Mt 9:36, where we read: 'When he saw the crowds, he had compassion for them, because they were harassed and helpless, like sheep without a shepherd.' I heard the Rev Ken Wilson, one of the leaders of the Vineyard fellowship in the US, speaking in a very moving way about how he had asked God to enable him to share in his heart for the lost. As a result the Lord gave him such a powerful awareness of Christ's thirst on the cross, a thirst not for water but for souls, that he went out into the streets to evangelise the homeless and down-and-outs. We need that kind of zeal in order to go searching for the prodigal sons and daughters of our time.

Secondly, we need to realise that a profound reorientation is underway, one that is moving clergy and lay people, alike, away from a maintenance to a missionary model of church.[14] Not only

14. Robert S. Rivers CSP, *From Maintenance to Mission: Evangelization and the Revitalization of the Parish* (New York: Paulist Press, 2005); Michael Sweeney OP, Sherry Anne Weddell, *The Parish: Mission or Maintenance?* (Colorado Springs: The Catherine of Siena Institute, 2000).

will it require a fundamental change in our way of thinking, it will also need to find expression in appropriate structural and practical innovations. The transition from the old to the new will be so demanding and painful that it will inevitably evoke a good deal of resistance, but it will also be tremendously worthwhile.

Thirdly, every diocese needs a well resourced office for the new evangelisation. Every parish needs to have a purpose or mission statement which includes a reference to the new evangelisation. I also believe that parish councils need to have an evangelisation committee which intentionally targets, if needs be with help from the diocesan office, the three different categories of people already mentioned. They can do this, for example, by providing training and showing them how to put on such things as Life in the Spirit Seminars, the different types of Alpha course, the Rite of Christian Initiation of Adults (RCIA), Cursillo weekends or parish missions. Surely there is a particular need to focus on young adults, i.e. 18-35 year olds, many of whom are drifting away from the church.

Fourthly, we witness to Christ by means of a Christian life well lived. By bearing silent witness, said Pope Paul VI in *EN* par. 21, 'these Christians will inevitably arouse a spirit of enquiry in those who see their way of life. Why are they like this? Why do they live this way? Why are they among us? Witness of this kind constitutes in itself a proclamation of the good news, silent but strong and effective.' This form of evangelisation is dealt with in *RM* par. 42, where we read: 'The evangelical witness which the world finds most appealing is that of concern for people, and of charity toward the poor, the weak and those who suffer. The complete generosity underlying this attitude and these actions stands in marked contrast to human selfishness. It raises precise questions which lead to God and to the gospel. A commitment to peace, justice, human rights and human promotion is also a witness to the gospel when it is a sign of concern for persons and is directed toward integral human development.'

Fifthly, all of us as individuals need to develop the courage and skill to engage in one-to-one evangelisation both within and outside our family circle. Par. 905 of the *Catechism of the Catholic Church* (hereafter *CCC*) says: 'Witness of life is not the sole element in the apostolate; the true apostle is on the lookout for occasions of announcing Christ by word, either to unbelievers or to the faithful.' As Pope Paul VI said in *EN* par. 46, 'Side by side with the collective proclamation of the gospel, the other form of evangelisation, the person-to-person one, remains valid and important.' It is a matter of seeing openings and knowing how to raise meaning of life topics such as, what do you think happens after death? We need to know and share the core message of Christianity. One way of doing this in a non-preachy way is to give our own testimony. I think that each of us should write and commit to memory a brief account of our religious awakening. It should describe three things: what you were like before the awakening occurred, the religious experience itself, and the effect it had on your life.

Sixthly, in *NMI* pars. 54-56, Pope John Paul II pointed out that we can evangelise by means of inter-religious dialogue, i.e. a relationship of openness and exchange with other philosophies, cultures and religions. In *EE* par. 55 he stated: 'As is the case with the overall commitment to the "new evangelisation", so too proclaiming the gospel of hope calls for the establishment of a profound and perceptive inter-religious dialogue, particularly with Judaism and with Islam.' In *NMI* par. 56, the Holy Father explained: 'Dialogue, however, cannot be based on religious indifferentism, and we Christians are in duty bound, while engaging in dialogue, to bear clear witness to the hope that is within us (cf 1 Pet 3:15) ... As the recent Declaration *Dominus Jesus* stressed, this cannot be the subject of a dialogue understood as negotiation, as if we considered it a matter of mere opinion: rather, it is a grace which fills us with joy, a message which we have a duty to proclaim.' For example, one could imagine that a Christian could have a fruitful dialogue with either Jews or Moslems about the identity and role of Jesus Christ.

Seventhly, we know that not only did Jesus demonstrate the truth of what he preached by means of deeds of power such as healing, exorcism and miracle working, he commissioned the apostles and their successors to do the same in his name. Thanks to the revival of the charisms in the contemporary church, many Christians can manifest the presence of the risen Lord by means of supernatural deeds. Belgian Cardinal Godfried Danneels has written a very interesting article entitled, 'The Charisms and the

New Evangelisation' in which he maintains that in times of crisis, such as the one we are living through, the Spirit multiplies his gifts.[15] From this point onwards, this book will concentrate on this seventh point.

SOME CONDITIONS NECESSARY FOR EFFECTIVE EVANGELISATION

It is clear from the New Testament, church teaching and lived experience that certain conditions are necessary for effective evangelisation to take place. Only three of them will be mentioned here.

a) The Power of the Holy Spirit

When one reads about the two outpourings of the Spirit on the apostles and disciples in Acts 2:1-41 and 4:23-31 it becomes obvious that there will be no effective evangelisation without the power of the Holy Spirit. As the psalmist wrote, 'Unless the Lord build, they labour in vain who build' (Ps 127:1). Both saints and popes have underlined this point. For instance, in 1656 St Vincent de Paul, founder of the Congregation of the Mission, said towards the end of his life, 'Neither philosophy, theology or discourses influence souls. It is essential that Jesus Christ be intimately united with us or we with him; that we operate in him and he in us; that we speak like him and in his spirit as he himself was in his Father and preached the doctrine taught him by the Father.'[16] Paul VI said something similar in EN par. 75. His wonderful words are well worth quoting at length: 'Evangelisation will never be possible without the action of the Holy Spirit ... Techniques of evangelisation are good, but even the most advanced ones could not replace the gentle action of the Spirit. The most perfect preparation of the evangeliser has no effect without the Holy Spirit. Without the Holy Spirit the most convincing dialectic has no power over the heart of man. Without him the most highly developed schemas resting on a sociological or psychological basis are quickly seen to be quite valueless ... It must be said that the Holy Spirit is the principal

---

15. *Goodnews* (Jan/Feb 2007), 6-7.
16. Andre Dodin CM, *Vincent de Paul and Charity: A Contemporary Portrait of his Life and Apostolic Spirit* (New York: New City Press, 1992), 81.

agent of evangelisation: it is he who impels each individual to proclaim the gospel, and it is he who in the depths of consciences causes the word of salvation to be accepted and understood ... Through the Holy Spirit the gospel penetrates to the heart of the world, for it is he who causes people to discern the signs of the times, signs willed by God, which evangelisation reveals and puts to use within history.' Members of the contemporary Pentecostal and Charismatic Movements maintain that 'baptism in the Spirit' is necessary for evangelisation in power, e.g. with associated healings miracles and deliverance from evil spirits. This controversial subject will be examined in chapter six.

b) Loving community

In 1976 Cardinal Suenens of Malines in Belgium hosted an ecumenical conference in his residence. One of the speakers was Graham Pulkinham, an Episcopal priest from the Church of the Holy Redeemer in Houston, Texas. That same year his church had been nominated by *Time* magazine as the 'best' in the United States. At one point during the conference he was invited by the Cardinal to speak about his experiences. He described how he had taken over a church that was dying, and how it was turned around as a result of an outpouring of the Spirit and his gifts. He went on to tell his audience about the commitment of the parishioners to prayer. He said that many of the men used gather early in the morning to pray before going to work. Then he went on to say something unforgettable to this listener. He stated that there could be no effective evangelisation in the power and gifts of the Holy Spirit without unity of mind and heart. Then he opened and read Acts 4:32-36, 'All the believers were one in heart and mind. No one claimed that any of his possessions was his own, but they shared everything they had. With great power the apostles continued to testify to the resurrection of the Lord Jesus, and much grace was upon them all. There were no needy persons among them. For from time to time those who owned lands or houses sold them, brought the money from the sales and put it at the apostle's feet, and it was distributed to anyone as he had need.' Afterwards he commented on the passage. He invited those present to notice that it was an idealised picture of the New Testament church. It was mostly about a unity of mind and heart which was expressed in a community of goods. But he said that his audience should notice how verse thirty-three about evangelisation: 'With great power the apostles gave their testimony to the resurrection of the Lord Jesus, and great grace was upon them all,' stuck up like a sore thumb in the middle of a passage about unity and sharing. Pulkingham observed, 'This may not be strictly logical from a literary point of view. But it is absolutely correct from a theological and experiential perspective. Effective evangelisation needs to be rooted in, and energised by a united community which acts as the icon of the good news message being preached.' Because unity of mind and heart is essential for effective evangelisation, every parish, community, and Christian group needs to deal with any negative attitudes and feelings which are inimical to that unity. The extent to which they are unacknowledged and left unresolved is the extent to which the Holy Spirit and his gifts will be quenched in the community. It is surely significant that St Paul situates his discussion of the gifts of the Spirit in 1 Cor 12:8-10, and Rom 12:4-12 within a discussion of the community as the body of Christ. The more the community is united in love the more it will be enabled to evangelise.

It is worth mentioning in this context that unity is not only necessary within churches, but also between churches (cf *EN* par. 77, & *RM* pars. 26, 51). In the late nineties I participated in ecumenical discussions in Northern Ireland. Eventually we published a pamphlet entitled, *Evangelicals and Catholics Together in Ireland*. In a section entitled, 'We witness together,' our committee wrote: 'The teaching of our Lord is unmistakable. The credibility of his mission in the world (and in Ireland in particular) is dependent upon the unity and love of his disciples as expressed in Jesus' prayer in John 17, "May they all be one; as you Father are in me, and I in you, so also may they be in us, that the world may believe that you sent me". This same connection between unity and witness is strongly echoed in Acts 4:32-36. The one Christ and one mission include many other Christians, as in Eastern Orthodox Churches and among those not commonly identified as Evangelical. All Christians are encompassed in the prayer, "May they all be one." It is thus that we are to "stand firm in one spirit, contending as one man for the faith of the gospel" (Phil 1:27).'[17]

17. (Dublin: ECT, 1998), 11-12.

The church is an oasis of community within a society where social cohesion seems to be weakening all the time. In 1887 Ferdinand Tonnies, a German sociologist, contrasted social relationships in traditional rural societies with those in modern industrial ones. He saw *Gemeinschaft* (traditional society) as intimate and positive, and *Gesellschaft* (modern society) as impersonal and negative. In small-scale societies everyone knows everyone else, the social order is seen as stable and the culture as homogeneous. When I was in rural Nigeria I noticed that this was the nature of society there. In large urban areas, such as Western cities, life is faster and more competitive, and relationships are seen as more superficial, transitory, and anonymous.[18] In 1893 Emile Durkheim made a similar distinction. In modern societies in contrast to traditional ones, he argued, the highly complex division of labour resulted in 'organic' as opposed to 'mechanical' solidarity. Different specialisations in employment and social roles created dependencies that tied people to one another, since people no longer could count on filling all of their needs by themselves (i.e. *Gesellschaft*). He felt that societies of this kind tend to suffer from *anomie*, i.e. a condition which results from the disintegration of a commonly accepted set of norms. He argued, quite rightly I think, that it made suicide more likely. In recent years, sociologists have talked about social capital, i.e. connections within and between social networks as well as connections among individuals. In his book *Bowling Alone*, Robert Putnam argued that in Western countries social capital has plummeted, thereby impoverishing our lives and communities.[19] Clearly observations of this kind are generalised and a bit abstract, but they have considerable relevance where evangelisation in contemporary society is concerned.

I can recall visiting a vibrant Protestant church in Belfast city in Northern Ireland a few years ago. I was very impressed by the fact that there were so many young adults in attendance. I asked the pastor what was the secret. He said that from a Christian point of view it would seem that three B's are involved in the

---

18. 'Gemeinschaft and Gesellschaft', *The Fontana Dictionary of Modern Thought*, ed, Allan Bullock & Oliver Stallybrass (London: Fontana Books, 1977), 256-257.
19. (New York: Simon & Shuster, 2000).

lives of Christians. Traditionally there was the B of right belief. That was followed by the B of right behaviour. Finally, there was the B of belonging. He said that in secular, postmodern society, where individualism is rampant and social alienation is common, people have an overriding need for a feeling of unconditional belonging. Arguably this is the essence of effective pre-evangelisation. Religious people are, literally, those who are bound together by a common experience of a love that simultaneously connects them to one another, to their deepest identities and ultimately to God. If the spiritual pilgrims of our day have a sense of belonging within a caring Christian community, they will be more likely to discover who they are and what they want. They will also be more open to accept the Christian beliefs that inform that community. It is only within this loving context that the issue of right behaviour can be tackled. Ideally, right action should be an expression of a sense of Christian belonging and belief, rather that a dutiful substitute for them both, as was sometimes the case in the past. I suspect that one reason why the Alpha course is so effective is the fact that it creates a sense of belonging by means of the meal that often precedes the teaching at the meeting.

c) Intercession and spiritual warfare

In Neh 2:17-20 and 4:5-17 there is a very interesting account of how the prophet Nehemiah was led by God to re-build the walls of Jerusalem. This story, as St Francis of Assisi realised so well,[20] has a metaphorical meaning. Jerusalem is the church which will be re-built by means of the new evangelisation. What is significant about the passage is the fact that only half of the volunteers seemed to be involved in the re-building, while the other half were devoted to vigilant awareness of the possible attacks of their enemies. Evangelisation that seeks to rebuild the church has to be supported, firstly by intercession. I got an insight into what this might involve at the Ecumenical conference referred to above which was hosted by Cardinal Suenens in Malines. Towards the end of the proceedings he opened Is 62:6-7 and said it was about the need for persistent intercessory prayer on behalf of the church: 'I have posted watchmen on your walls, O

20. *The Life of St Francis of Assisi*, pp. 18; 23-25.

Jerusalem; they will never be silent day or night. You who call on the Lord, give yourselves no rest, and give him no rest till he establishes Jerusalem and makes her the praise of the earth.' Paul linked intercession and evangelisation when he wrote in Eph 6:18-19, 'Pray in the Spirit on all occasions with all kinds of prayers and requests. With this in mind, be alert and always keep on praying for all the saints.' Our intercession needs to be frequent, intense, associated with fasting, and within a context of worship.

Whenever we attempt to extend God's kingdom by means of evangelisation, the devil will inevitably seek to disrupt our efforts in all sorts of devious ways. As Paul reminds us, 'our struggle is not with flesh and blood but with principalities, with the powers, with the worldly rulers of this present darkness, with the evil spirits in the heavens' (Eph 6:12). Intercessors and evangelists alike, need a gift of discernment in order to, 'test the spirits to see whether they are from God' (1 John 4:1). Furthermore, they need to act defensively by, 'taking the shield of faith, with which you can quench all the flaming darts of the evil one' (Eph 6:16), and to act offensively with 'the sword of the Spirit which is the word of God' (Eph 6:17). They do both in the knowledge that, 'We destroy arguments and every proud obstacle to the knowledge of God, and take every thought captive to obey Christ' (2 Cor 10:5).

d) Personal holiness

Pope John Paul II made it very clear that evangelisation will not be effective unless those who conduct it are themselves holy people, i.e. filled, guided and empowered by the Holy Spirit. In *RM* par. 90 the pontiff wrote: 'The universal call to holiness is closely linked to the universal call to mission. Every member of the faithful is called to holiness and to mission.' Some time ago when I was prayerfully preparing a homily on the call to holiness, these words came to me: 'I am the Lord your God, the holy one. My people, do not compromise with sin. If there is mortal sin in your life, do not deny or excuse it. Repent, receive my forgiveness, avoid the first stirrings of temptation and believe that I will deliver you from the web of evil that holds you captive. If there is venial sin in your life, do not tolerate it. Be aware that secret and unrepented sin in the lives of those who believe in me is the greatest single obstacle to the work of my Spirit. I want you to be holy, I want you to turn away from the ways of the world. I call on you to root out your sins, great and small alike. Be assured that I will not only enlighten your heart to know your sins, I will enable you to turn away from them by a great and liberating outpouring of my grace. Be holy as I am holy. There is no substitute for this holiness. There is no plan, effort or activity, no matter how well intentioned, which will accomplish my purposes if you are not holy like me. When your heart is cleansed, my Spirit will pray ardently within you, it will guide you in ways you have not known, it will empower and protect you from the deceptions of the evil one. It will fill you with my joy. I weep for the world and my church. There are many, who because of their great and repeated sins, are travelling the wide road that leads to perdition. Call them to repentance, before it is too late, so that they may come back to me. I promise you that many of them will heed your words when they see my holiness shining forth in your lives. My people, the time of breach-mending is at hand. I will enable you to re-build the walls of Jerusalem. I am about to accomplish a great work of restoration.'

CONCLUSION

To make the transition from maintenance to mission is going to require a lot of change, effort and commitment. In *EE* par. 49, John Paul II wrote: 'Europe calls out for credible evangelisers, whose lives, in communion with the cross and resurrection of Christ, radiate the beauty of the gospel.' Such evangelisers must be properly trained. Now more than ever a missionary consciousness is needed in all Christians, beginning with bishops, priests, deacons, consecrated persons, catechists and teachers of religion: 'All the baptized, since they are witnesses of Christ, should receive a training appropriate to their circumstances, not only so that their faith does not wither for lack of care in a hostile environment such as the secularist world, but also so that their witness to the gospel will receive strength and inspiration.' The implication of this is that we will need to establish and resource schools of evangelisation. Happily, there are already a number of them in these islands.

CHAPTER TWO

The Gifts of the Spirit and Evangelisation in the New Testament

In view of the fact that Jesus was the evangeliser *par excellence*, this chapter will begin by indicating that following his baptism in the Spirit, Jesus received revelation from his Father, that he proclaimed that revelation is his preaching and teaching and demonstrated its truth in many ways, especially by deeds of power. It seems quite clear in the gospels that Jesus commissioned his disciples to do the same in his name. This chapter will go on to examine a well known passage in 1 Cor 12:8-10 in order to establish whether Christ's template of revelation, proclamation and demonstration finds an echo in Paul's understanding of the charisms.

JESUS THE EVANGELISER PAR EXCELLANCE

Speaking about the baptism of Jesus, Pope Paul VI observed in his encyclical *On Christian Joy*, 'Jesus ... knows that he is loved by his Father. When he is baptised on the banks of the Jordan, this love, which is present from the first moment of his conception, *is manifested* [my italics]. He knows that he is God's Son, the Beloved, who enjoys God's favour. This certitude is inseparable from the consciousness of Jesus. It is a presence which never leaves him all alone. It is an intimate knowledge which fills him ... For Jesus it is not a question of a passing awareness. It is the reverberation in his human consciousness of the love that he has always known as God in the bosom of the Father.'[1] Pope Paul's use of the word 'manifested' is ambiguous, manifested to whom? the consciousness of Jesus? the onlookers? or both? Pope Leo XIII spoke about the baptism of Jesus in par. 4 of *Divinum*

---

1. Section three: 'Joy According to the New Testament.' http://www.vatican.va/holy_father/paul_vi/apost_exhortations/documents/hf_p-vi_exh_19750509_gaudete-in-domino_en.html (accessed May 2nd 2008)

Illud Munus (1987) where he said: 'At this time, then [that is, at his baptism], he was pleased to prefigure his church.'[2] John Paul II also talked about the baptism of Jesus in pars. 16-22 of his encyclical *Dominum et Vivificantem* but did not address this specific topic. Pope Benedict XVI says that we can say nothing about Jesus' psychological state at his baptism.[3] Furthermore he denies that it had a vocational element.[4] It would seem therefore, that Jesus' identity and calling were revealed to the onlookers, but not to him personally because, as God, he was already aware of both. It should be said that a number of reputable scripture and patristic scholars, such as C. H. Dodd, Oscar Cullman, Killian McDonnell[5] and Raniero Cantalamessa, would not take as emphatic a position as Benedict. For instance, commenting on the relevant baptismal scripture texts, papal preacher Raniero Cantalamessa says: 'We are talking about a functional newness, that is in the mission; not a metaphysical one, in the depths of the person. It manifests itself by grandiose and immediate effects: miracles, preaching with authority, the ushering in of the kingdom of God, victory over demons.'[6]

Cantalamessa links the baptism of Jesus and the coming of the Spirit at Pentecost when he says: 'The anointing of Christ was an anointing for our benefit in the sense that it was intended for us.'[7] He goes on to say a little later: 'At Pentecost and, before that, in the paschal mystery, Jesus poured out on the church that Spirit which he had received from the Father at his baptism.'[8]

From the time of his baptism onwards, Jesus began to 'do and to teach' (Acts 1:1). In John's gospel, however, Jesus testified to the fact that the things he said and did as a man, were rooted in revelation from the Father. Here are a number of instances. In Jn 5:19, 30 he said, 'Very truly, I tell you, the Son can do nothing

2. http://www.ewtn.com/library/encyc/l13divin.htm (accessed 8 April 2006)
3. *Jesus of Nazareth* (London: Bloomsbury, 2007), 24.
4. Ibid., 23-24.
5. *The Baptism of Jesus in the Jordan* (Collegeville, Minnesota: The Liturgical Press, 1996), 5-6.
6. Raniero Cantalamessa, *The Holy Spirit in the Life of Jesus* (Collegeville, Minnesota: The Liturgical Press, 1994),12.
7. Ibid., 12-13.
8. Ibid., 13.

on his own, but only what he sees the Father doing; for whatever the Father does, the Son does likewise ...' 'I can do nothing on my own. As I hear, I judge; and my judgement is just, because I seek to do not my own will but the will of him who sent me.' Some time later he said in Jn 12:49, 'For I have not spoken on my own, but the Father who sent me has himself given me a commandment about what to say and what to speak.'

These verses, and similar ones in Jn 14:24, 31, indicate that everything Jesus said and did in the course of his evangelisation was a manifestation of the action of God the Father in and through him. Three instances of the linkage between the proclamation and demonstration of the good news can be highlighted here. The first occurred when Jesus made his mission statement in his local synagogue. Lk 4:16-30 tells us that he was providentially handed a scroll which contained the words of Is 62:1-2. Jesus proceeded to announce that he had been anointed by the Holy Spirit to bring good news to outcasts, sinners, and those who knew their radical need of God's grace. Whereas the Jewish authorities said that such people were under a curse of condemnation for neither knowing or keeping the law (see Jn 7:49), Jesus announced the jubilee time of God's unconditional grace when the debt due to sin would be forgiven and forgotten. What is very interesting about this mission statement is the fact that it includes a reference to the demonstration of the power of the Spirit in the form of 'recovery of sight for the blind'.

The second significant text that links the words and supernatural actions of Jesus is to be found in Matthew's gospel. St John the Baptist was in prison. Apparently he was having doubts about Jesus' identity and role. After all, he himself had expected a prophet of eschatological wrath and judgement. So he sent messengers to ask Jesus whether he was the promised messiah or not. Jesus gave an indirect answer when he responded: 'Go back and report to John what you hear and see: The blind receive sight, the lame walk, those who have leprosy are cured, the deaf hear, the dead are raised [demonstration], and the good news is preached to the poor [proclamation]' Mt 11:4-5. In other words, he was fulfilling the messianic texts in Is 35:5, 6, 61:1 and his own mission statement. He was proclaiming the good news to sinners and his deeds of power were the good news in action, the in-breaking of God's merciful kingdom in their lives.[9] There is an echo of that response in Jn 14:11: 'Believe me when I say that I am in the Father and the Father is in me; or at least believe on the evidence of the miracles themselves.'

The third significant incident took place after the death and resurrection of Jesus. We know that during his public ministry, he had authorised the apostles to proclaim and demonstrate the coming of the kingdom of God: 'And he called the twelve together and gave them power and authority over all demons and to cure diseases, and he sent them out to preach the kingdom of God and to heal' Lk 9:1-2. Immediately before his ascension to the Father he renewed that mandate when he gave the apostles the great commission. 'Go into the world and preach the good news to all creation' Mk 16:15. Then he promised them that, like him, they would be able to demonstrate the reality of the message of good news by deeds of power: 'In my name they will drive out demons ... they will place their hands on sick people and they will get well' Mk 15:17-18. Whether Mark wrote this ending or not, is not really important. One way or the other, the inspired text is an echo of a promise made by Jesus in Jn 14:12: 'I tell you the truth, anyone who has faith in me will do what I have been doing. He will do even greater things than these, because I am going to the Father.' Contrary to those who say that the phrase 'greater things' referred only to effective preaching, Raymond Brown maintains in his commentary on this remarkable verse that it not only refers to effective proclamation, it also refers to supernatural demonstration by means of deeds of power.[10] Francis J. Maloney concurs in his commentary on the fourth gospel.[11]

There is clear evidence in the Acts, that the apostles carried out the Lord's instructions. They did 'the greater things'

---

9. Jesus made a similar point in Jn 10:25, 'The miracles I do in my Father's name speak for me.' As Par. 551 of the *Catechism of the Catholic Church* points out, 'His (Jesus') deeds, miracles, and words all revealed that, "in him the fullness of deity dwells bodily" (Col 2:9).'

10. *The Gospel According to John*, vol. 2, XIII-XXI, *The Anchor Bible*, vol 29a (Garden City, New York: Doubleday, 1970), 622.

11. Francis J. Moloney SDB, *The Gospel of John*, vol 4, Sacra Pagina, ed., Daniel J Harrington SJ, (Collegeville: The Liturgical Press, 1998), 399-400.

promised by Jesus when they proclaimed the good news in words and demonstrated it in mighty deeds. As Acts 2:43 testifies, 'Many wonders and signs were done through the apostles.' On Pentecost day, St Peter made as many as 3,000 converts. When the early church experienced persecution the disciples prayed for a second, little Pentecost in Acts 4:29-30. What is significant is the fact that they asked for the power of effective proclamation and demonstration in the Holy Spirit. 'Enable your servants,' they prayed, 'to speak your word with great boldness. Stretch out your hand to heal and perform miraculous signs and wonders through the name of your holy servant Jesus.' Later St Paul echoed that exact point in Rom 15:18-19, 'I will not venture to speak of anything except what Christ has accomplished through me in leading the Gentiles to obey God by what I have said and done – by the power of signs and miracles, through the power of the Spirit.'

It could be said, with theological justification, that what the apostles and disciples did to evangelise in the name of Jesus is to a certain degree a template for what modern day Christians can and should also do. In St Eudes's book, *The Kingdom of God in the Souls of Christians* (1637), it says, 'We can say that any true Christian, who is a member of Jesus Christ, and who is united to him by his grace, *continues* and *completes*, [my italics] through all the actions that he carries out in the spirit of Christ, the actions that Jesus Christ accomplished during the time of his temporary life on earth. So that when a Christian prays, he continues and fulfils the prayer that Jesus Christ offered on earth. Whenever he works, he continues and fulfils the laborious life of Jesus Christ. Whenever he relates to his or her neighbour in a spirit of charity, then he continues and fulfils the relational life of Jesus Christ. Whenever he eats or rests in a Christian manner, he continues and fulfils the subjection that Jesus Christ wished to have these necessities. The same can be said of any other action that is carried out in a Christian manner.'[12] Although Eudes did not mention charismatic activity in support of evangelisation, his general theological principle would surely imply it.

---

12. *Berulle and the French School: Selected Writings*, ed. W. Thompson, (New York: Paulist Press, 1989), 296.

ST PAUL ON GIFTS OF REVELATION, PROCLAMATION, AND DEMONSTRATION

This book has reached the point where the focus moves more specifically to Paul's list of nine charisms in 1 Cor 12:8-10. A number of introductory comments can be made. Firstly, there are other gift lists besides this one, notably in 1 Cor 12:28, Eph 4:11-12 and Rom 12:6-8. There seems to be general agreement among scholars that these lists are intended to be exemplary rather than exhaustive. Secondly, although it is unlikely that Paul had any conscious classification of the gifts in mind, there may be an implicit one. A number of contemporary scripture scholars have referred to the main typologies that have been proposed by academics, in their commentaries.[13] For instance, Gordon Fee refers W. R. Jones's typically Pentecostalist list of three groups of three gifts in 'The Nine Gifts of the Holy Spirit.'[14] They are,

1. *Illumination:* wisdom, knowledge, discernment.
2. *Communication:* prophecy, tongues, interpretation of tongues.
3. *Action:* faith, miracles, healings.

At this point, a slightly different classification will be proposed. Although it has not been described in exactly the same form by any scripture scholar, the aim here is to show that it is justifiable on exegetical and theological grounds. As will be evident in chapter three, in general terms it happens to be similar to the classification proposed by St Thomas Aquinas.

1. *Revelation:* wisdom and knowledge, prophecy, and discernment of spirits.

---

13. Gordon Fee, *The First Epistle to the Corinthians* (Grand Rapids, Ml: Eerdmans, 1987), 590-591; Paul Njiru, *Charisms and the Holy Spirit's Activity in the Body of Christ: An Exegetical-Theological Study of 1 Corinthians 12:4-11 and Romans 12:6-8* (Rome: Gregorian University, 2002), 130-132; Raymond Collins, *First Corinthians* (Collegeville: The Liturgical Press, 2007), 451. Collins says, that rather than arranging the gifts in a triad of triads, they are arranged on an A-B-A basis, with two gifts, wisdom, and knowledge, at the beginning; five gifts, faith, healings, miracle working, prophecy, and discernment of spirits in the middle; and two gifts, tongues and interpretation of tongues, at the end.

14. *Pentecostal Doctrine*, ed. Percy Brewster (Cheltenham: Grenehurst, 1976), 46-71.

2. *Proclamation:* the utterance of wisdom, the utterance of knowledge, utterances in tongues, interpretation of tongues.
3. *Demonstration:* faith, healings (possibly exorcisms), and miracles.

GIFTS OF REVELATION

In English the words 'reveal' and 'revelation' are both derived from the Latin, *revelare* meaning 'to unveil' or to manifest that which is hidden. Their Hebrew and Greek equivalents, *gala* and *apokalypto* respectively, mean much the same. Morton Kelsey has pointed out in his *Encounter with God: A Theology of Christian Experience*, that the New Testament abounds in revelatory experiences.[15] This way of knowing can lead, by means of such things as dreams and visions, to a primal, prerational awareness of the presence of God. It is reminiscent of the ecstatic experiences of the *nabi*, prophets who often expressed in words what had first been revealed to them in prerational ways. As George Montague has observed, 'In Old Testament prophecy the pendulum swings between the ecstatic, non-rational, pre-conceptual element and the intelligible, rational, spoken word. But in either case prophecy is essentially a gift of inspiration.'[16] Because most post-Enlightenment people, who have been tainted by Cartesian and Kantian rationalism of a subjectivist kind, and the closed worldview of Newtonian science, do not believe in the possibility of this form of supernatural communication, they would have difficulty in accepting the validity of the notion of openness to supernatural revelation from God.

a) The Relationship between Wisdom and Knowledge
In 1 Cor 12:8 St Paul refers to charisms of the *utterance* of wisdom and knowledge. That would indicate that they are proclamatory rather than revelatory gifts. St Augustine, one of the greatest of the Fathers of the Church, commented on these gifts on a number of occasions in his *De Trinitate*. Having referred to 1 Cor 12:8,

---

15. Appendix, Parts 1 & 2, *Encounter With God: A Theology of Christian Experience* (London: Hodder & Stoughton, 1974), 242-245.
16. *The Spirit and His Gifts: The Biblical Background of Spirit-baptism, Tongue-speaking, and Prophecy* (New York: Paulist Press/Deus Books, 1974), 33.

he said that while Paul clearly distinguished one gift from another he did not clarify in what way they differed. Augustine said in book 12, par. 22: 'wisdom belongs to contemplation, knowledge to action.'[17] Later, in books 13, par. 24, and 14, par. 3 he said that: 'wisdom is attributed to divine things and knowledge to human.'[18] What is interesting about Augustine's comments on 1 Cor 12:8 is the fact that he seemed to ignore the proclamatory aspect of the two gifts by focusing on their revelatory nature. As such they have more to do with the first two gifts in the traditional list in Is 11:2. It is probable, therefore, that the *utterance* of wisdom and knowledge is the proclamation of what has already been revealed by means of the related gifts. While it would be a mistake to try to give each of the words a precise meaning, it could be said that wisdom has more to do with deep, directional insight into the purposes of Christ, whereas knowledge has to do with a deep, informative insight into the person of God in Christ.

b) The Gift of Wisdom

While Paul's understanding of the gift of wisdom was rooted in the gift mentioned in Is 11:2, and elsewhere in the Old Testament, it was more directly influenced by the mystery of Christ. Paul acknowledged that his preaching was 'not in plausible words of wisdom.' Nevertheless, he called his proclamation of the gospel the 'wisdom of God' just as Christ himself is 'the wisdom of God' (1 Cor 1:24, 30, 2:1-5, 7). In a passage redolent with orthodox Christian Gnosticism, Paul said that the Spirit searches the depths of God. 'We have received,' he says, 'the Spirit which is from God that we may understand what God has freely given us' (1 Cor 2:12). A little later he says: 'For who has known the mind of the Lord that he may instruct him? But we have the mind of Christ' (1 Cor 2:16). Paul's ethic flows from his doctrinal faith and can be summed up in the words: 'be guided by the Spirit' (Gal 5:18). It is not surprising therefore, that he prayed that the believers would 'find out what pleases the Lord' (Eph 5:10). He hoped that they would 'abound more and more

---

17. Translated and introduced by Edmund Hill OP, (New York: New City Press, 1991), 334.
18. Ibid., 371.

in knowledge and depth of insight, so that they may be able to discern what is best' (Phil 1:9). Finally, Paul testified in Col 1:9-12: 'Since the day we heard about you, we have not stopped praying for you and asking God to fill you with the knowledge of his will through all spiritual wisdom and understanding. And we pray this in order that you may live a life worthy of the Lord and may please him in every way: bearing fruit in every good work, growing in the knowledge of God.' The Apostle James said at the beginning of his epistle that if anyone needed this kind of practical wisdom they should pray for it with expectant faith (Jas 1:5-8).

c) The Gift of Knowledge
When Paul refers to knowledge in 1 Cor 12:9 the Greek word he uses is *gnosis*. The gift of knowledge seems to be a contemplative grace which enables those who receive it to understand the alive and active word of God, and ultimately the mystery of the God-self. In 2 Cor 10:5 the apostle talks about diabolical obstacles 'that set themselves up against the knowledge of God.' In Col 2:5 he expresses the desire that members of the community, 'May have the full riches of complete understanding, in order that they may know the mystery of God, namely, Christ, in whom are hidden all the treasures of wisdom and knowledge.' Over the centuries the church has recommended the practice of engaging in *Lectio Divina* precisely because it enables people, in the words of St Ignatius of Loyola 'to have an intimate knowledge of Jesus, who became human for us.'[19] Surely Ignatius was also referring to the gift of knowledge when he said, 'It is not knowing much, but realising and relishing things interiorly, that contents and satisfies the soul.'[20] This notion is consistent with what is said in Is 6b-8a and Jer 33:3.

d) The so-called 'Word of Knowledge'
Although some Pentecostals and Charismatics think that the so-

19. *Spiritual Exercises*, par. 233.
20. *Spiritual Exercises*, annotation two. In his 'Sermon and Collation for the Feast of Pentecost,' St. Thomas wrote in similar vein when he said: 'Without a feeling [*sensu*] for the truth, no one speaks what is true. In like manner, the Holy Spirit makes all the saints speak copiously, and for this reason Gregory says: 'Those whom he fills, he makes wise".'

called 'word of knowledge' is an aspect of the utterance of knowledge, scripture scholars are inclined to think that it is really a form of revelatory prophecy.[21] For instance, in his commentary on 1 Corinthians, Gordon Fee says that the word of knowledge is, 'A supernatural endowment of knowledge, factual information that could not otherwise have been known without the Spirit's aid, *such as frequently occurs in the prophetic tradition*' [my italics].[22]

Words of knowledge can be received in different ways, such as a mental image, an inner word or a combination of both. However they are received they can be invaluable in different ministry situations. Here are four examples: Firstly, in the sacrament of reconciliation some priests will occasionally know a penitent's secret sins. This knowledge enables them to help him or her to make a good confession. John Wimber recounts how, during a flight, it was revealed to him that a fellow passenger was in an adulterous relationship.[23] When he spoke to the man in question about the affair, he had a life changing conversion experience. Secondly, the Lord can guide intercessory prayer in an inspired way by means of a word of knowledge. Thirdly, those who pray for inner healing are sometimes led by a word of knowledge to focus on a repressed memory. Fourthly, as the ministry of Kathryn Kuhlman and other well known healers have demonstrated, words of knowledge are sometimes granted to those praying for physical cures, particularly at healing services.

e) Discernment of Spirits

The discernment of Spirits in 1 Cor 12:10 is not so much about a generalised ability to distinguish inspirations that come from God from those that do not, as a God given charism which enables the gifted person to test the Spirits (1 Jn 4:1-6). He or she is able to identify which prophecies are prompted by the Spirit,

21 Pat Collins CM, 'ESP and Inspired Words of Knowledge,' *Mind and Spirit: Spirituality and Psychology in Dialogue* (Dublin: Columba, 2006), 91-112.

22. Fee, Gordon D., *op. cit.*, 592-593.

23. *Power Evangelism: Signs and Wonders Today* (London: Hodder & Stoughton, 1985), 44-46.

and which come from the person himself or herself, or even from the devil. In his commentary on this verse, St John Chrysostom said: 'What is, discerning of spirits? knowing who is spiritual, and who is not.'[24] There is an ambiguity in what he said: is he referring to prophecy in particular or to all kinds of promptings and inspiration? One way or the other, Paul says in 1 Cor 14:29 that discernment involves weighing up carefully what is said. In 1 Thess 5:19-21 we read: 'Do not quench the Spirit. Do not despise the words of prophets, but test everything; hold fast to what is good.'

GIFTS OF PROCLAMATION

It seems fairly obvious from the context in 1 Cor 12:8 that when St Paul talked about gifts of proclamation he was considering them more as a means of edifying the body of Christ, than as a means of evangelisation. However, it would be a mistake to create a false antithesis between the two activities. The community needed to be built up in order to carry out the great commission. He does refer to evangelisation in 1 Cor 14:22 were he says, 'Tongues then are a sign, not for believers but for unbelievers.'

a) The Utterance of Wisdom

This gift is a pedagogical ability which was given to some members of the community to edify and sanctify others.[25] The utterance of wisdom is rooted in the revelatory gifts which have already been described, but goes beyond them in so far as it enables those who have received it to speak in an anointed and effective way about the person and purposes of God. More often than not, this charism is granted to those engaged in evangelisation, especially apostles, prophets, preachers and teachers. Commenting on the utterance of wisdom, George Montague says, '...it seems that Paul is not discussing a stable gift, even less a stable office – there was no office of "wise men" in the

---

24. Homily 29, Homilies on First Corinthians http://www.newadvent.org/fathers/2201.htm (accessed May 10 2008)
25. Pat Collins 'The Gifts of Wisdom and Knowledge,' *Goodnews* (May/June 2005); C. M. Robeck Jr, 'Word of Wisdom,' *The New International Dictionary of the Pentecostal and Charismatic Movements,* 1200-1202.

early church – but rather simply a passing movement by the Holy Spirit whereby someone in the community is given a flash of insight into the living of the Christian life.'[26]

An example of this gift in action is provided in Acts 15:1-21 which describes how the first Council of Jerusalem discussed whether pagan converts to Christianity needed to be circumcised or not. James uttered a charismatic word of wisdom when he quoted from (Is 45:21; Jer 12:15; Amos 9:11, 12), and adjudicated that circumcision would not be necessary. The spontaneity of the inspiration is reminiscent of what Jesus said, e.g. 'When you are brought before synagogues, rulers and authorities, do not worry about how you will defend yourselves or what you will say, for the Holy Spirit will teach you at that time what you should say' (Lk 12:11-12).

b) The Utterance of Knowledge

The utterance of knowledge is similar to the utterance of wisdom.[27] It probably refers to an inspired insight into the Christian mystery which leads to the successful instruction of people. Arguably, the evangelistic efforts of anyone with the ministry of preacher or teacher, would be greatly enhanced by these charisms. Those of us who have heard people such as Fr Raniero Cantalamessa OFM Cap, Fr Jim Burke OP, Mr Jean Vanier, and Ms Francis Hogan either preach or teach would probably agree that their effectiveness is due to the fact that they are blessed with the charism of the utterance of knowledge. Speaking about the relationship between the utterance of wisdom and knowledge G. K. Barrett said in his commentary on 1 Corinthians: 'A word of wisdom would then represent a practical discourse, consisting mainly of ethical instruction and exhortation, and a word of knowledge is connected with practical matters.'[28]

---

26. *The Holy Spirit: Growth of a Biblical Tradition,* (NY: Paulist Press, 1976), 150.
27. Francis Martin, 'Word of Knowledge,' *The New International Dictionary of the Pentecostal and Charismatic Movements,* 823-825.
28. *A Commentary on the first Epistle to the Corinthians* (London: BNTC, 1968), 285.

c) Prophecy

The word 'prophet' is derived from the Greek *prophetes*, meaning interpreter, or spokesman.[29] In other words a prophet or prophetess is a person who speaks or acts in a revelatory way on God's behalf, under the inspiration of the Holy Spirit. It could be defined as an ability which is granted to a believer by the Spirit to speak forth words from God that do not come from the person's natural intelligence or knowledge. In *The New International Dictionary of the Pentecostal and Charismatic Movements* the gift of prophecy is described in these words: 'Prophecy has been alternatively identified as (1) an oracle, spontaneously inspired by the Holy Spirit and spoken in specific situations; (2) a form of expositional preaching from a biblical text; or (3) a public pronouncement of a moral or ethical nature that confronts society.'[30]

Pauline scholar George Montague says that prophecy is more a matter of 'forth-telling' than 'fore-telling.'[31] In other words the prophet or prophetess evaluates the signs of the times in terms of the mind and heart of God. They gain this insight as a result of an inspired vision, inner word, or dream. The scriptures are clear that prophecy as a spoken word is rooted in revelation. Although genuine prophecy is revelatory, it merely elucidates the implications of scriptural revelation, without adding to it. Because he valued prophecy more than any of the other gifts of the Spirit, it is not surprising that Paul spoke about it more than any of the other gifts, e.g. in 1 Thess 5:20; 1 Cor 11:4-5; 12-14; Rom 12:6; Eph 2:20; 3:5; 4:11; 1 Tim 1:18; 4:14. Paul says in 1 Cor 14:3, 'everyone who prophesies speaks to men for their edification, exhortation and comfort.' In contemporary terms it could be described as a matter of building up, stirring up and cheering up.

29. Pat Collins, 'Prophecy' *Goodnews* (Sept/Oct 2002), 3-4; 'Preparing to Prophecy' *Goodnews* (Nov/Dec 2004), 30-31.
30. Stanley M. Burgess, Eduard M. Van Der Maas, eds., (Grand Rapids, MI.: Zondervan, 2003), 999.
31. George Montague says this on page 30 of *The Holy Spirit and His Gifts*, referred to above. St Thomas says in the ST q. 171, a. 1, corpus, that 'to hold that men have no such foreknowledge of the future, but that they can acquire it by means of experience, wherein they are helped by their natural disposition, which depends on the perfection of man's imaginative power and the clarity of his understanding, is mistaken.'

There are a number of ways in which prophecy can do this. Firstly, it can take the form of a message which is spontaneously inspired by the Holy Spirit and spoken into a particular situation. Secondly, prophecy can take the form of inspired and inspiring preaching based on a scripture text. Thirdly, prophecy can take the form of a challenging public pronouncement on a moral or ethical issue that confronts current social values, e.g. many of the statements made by John Paul II about the culture of death. Fourthly, a person can either receive a personal word interiorly, or through someone else. Besides edifying the community, Paul said in 1 Cor 14:24-25 that the gift had the ability to evangelise people: 'If all prophesy, and an unbeliever or outsider enters, he is convicted by all, he is called to account by all, the secrets of his heart are disclosed; and so, falling on his face, he will worship God and declare that God is really among you.'

d) Utterance in Tongues and Interpretation of Tongues

Jerome Murphy-O Connor and Raymond Brown have both warned that present day Christians cannot be sure that they are interpreting texts about the charisms correctly.[32] Nowhere is that more true than in the case of praying and speaking in tongues. Paul seemed to make a distinction between these two forms. Firstly, there was non-conceptual, non imaginative *glossalalia* as private prayer.[33] Paul says that, 'For if I pray in a tongue, my spirit prays, but my mind is unfruitful' (1 Cor 14:14). Secondly, there seems to be a form of public utterance in tongues. It is not at all clear whether it is addressed to God or the people present. This kind of speaking in tongues seemed to be a sort of non-conceptual utterance of a prophetic kind. Speaking about this form of speaking in tongues, Paul advised that if someone made such a public utterance, the gathering should

---

32. *New Jerome Biblical Commentary*, eds, Raymond E. Brown, Joseph A. Fitzmyer, Roland E. Murphy (New Jersey: Prentice Hall, 1990), 810; *An Introduction to the New Testament* (New York: Doubleday, 1977), 532.

33. Pat Collins CM, 'Tongues and Contemplation,' *He Has Anointed Me* (Luton: New Life Publishing, 2004); 24-28. R. P. Spittler, 'Glossolalia,' *New International Dictionary of Pentecostal and Charismatic Movements*, 670-676; George Montague, *The Holy Spirit: Growth of a Biblical Tradition*, 155-156.

wait until there was an interpretation as opposed to a translation: 'Anyone who speaks in a tongue should pray that he may interpret what he says' (1 Cor 14:13). Conceivably the interpretation could take the form of a prayer, or 'some revelation, knowledge, prophecy or word of instruction' (1 Cor 14:6). As will be noted in chapters three and four, an utterance in tongues can take the form of *xenoglossi*, i.e. either an ability to speak foreign languages, or to be understood by foreigners when the speaker speaks in tongues. However, it is unlikely that Paul has this in mind in 1 Cor 12:10 because the utterances would not need to be interpreted if they were intelligible.

GIFTS OF DEMONSTRATION

a) The Charism of Faith

The most important reference to this charism is to be found in 1 Cor 12:9, where Paul says that to some is given 'faith by the same Spirit'. George Montague is representative of the shared opinion of scripture scholars when he writes, 'The gift of faith in 1 Cor 12:9 does not refer here to the faith that is necessary for salvation (Mk 16:16; Heb 11:6), but rather to a special intensity of faith for a specific need.'[34] Commentators down the centuries are agreed that Paul is not referring to saving faith, but rather to an exceptional form of expectant trust that leads to deeds of power.[35] In one of his 'Catechetical Lectures,' St Cyril of Jerusalem (c. 315-386 AD) said, 'The word "faith" has two meanings. First of all, it is concerned with doctrine and it denotes the assent of the soul to some truth … The word "faith" has a second meaning: it is a particular gift and grace of Christ. "To one is given through the Spirit the utterance of wisdom, and to another the utterance of knowledge, according to the same Spirit, to another faith by the

34. *The Holy Spirit: Growth of a Biblical Tradition*, 152.
35. William F. Orr and James Arthur Walther, *1 Corinthians, The Anchor Bible*, (New York: Doubleday, 1976), 282.; C. K. Barrett, *A Commentary on the First Epistle to the Corinthians*, (London: Adam & Charles Black, 1971), 285-286; D. A. Carson, *Showing the Spirit: A Theological Exposition of 1 Corinthians 12-14* (Grand Rapids: Baker Book House, 1987), 38-39; Hans Conzelman, *1 Corinthians: A Commentary on the First Epistle to the Corinthians* (Philadelphia: Fortress Press, 1975), 209; Arnold Bittlinger, *Gifts and Graces: A Commentary on 1 Corinthians 12-14* (London: Hodder & Stoughton, 1967), 32-34; Raymond Collins, *First Corinthians*, 454.

same spirit, to another gifts of healing" 1 Cor 12:8-9. Faith in the sense of a particular divine grace conferred by the Spirit is not primarily concerned with doctrine but with giving people powers which are quite beyond their capability.'[36]

The charism of faith is a gratuitous as opposed to a sanctifying grace, which is granted to some by the Holy Spirit. Rooted in the gifts of revelation, it enables them in particular situations, to discern with trusting conviction of a heartfelt and expectant kind that, in answer to a prayer of either petition or command, the unconditional mercy and love of God will be manifested through a deed of power such as an exorcism, healing, or miracle. Such edifying epiphanies of salvation are anticipations, in the present, of the future transformation of all things in the Second Coming of Christ.

As has been noted already, the charism of expectant faith is evoked by the charisms of revelation, especially prophetic words of knowledge. They reveal what God's will is, so that a person has no lingering doubts about the promises of God. Once he or she knows God's existential will, they can pray either a prayer of intercession (Mk 11:24), or command (Mk 11:23), with complete assurance. As 1 Jn 5:14 says, 'And this is the confidence we have in God, that if we ask for anything according to his will, he hears us. And if we know that he hears us in whatever we ask, we know that *we have obtained the requests* [my italics] made of him.' In other words, it is not a matter of praying with future hope, if what he or she asks for is in accordance with God's will. Rather, it is a matter of praying with present conviction because the person already knows that what he or she asks for is God's will. This writer has argued elsewhere that the charism of expectant faith is a prerequisite for the exercise of the charisms of power listed in 1 Cor 12:10 such as healing and miracle working.[37]

b) The Gift of Healings

If, more often than not, the charism of faith is rooted in the

---

36. *The Faith of the Early Fathers*, vol 1, (Collegeville: Liturgical Press, 1970), 352-353.
37. Pat Collins CM, *Expectant Faith* (Dublin: Columba, 1997); 'The Prayer of Command,' *Prayer in Practice* (New York: Orbis, 2000), 148-166.

charisms of revelation, it can find expression in the gift of healings. Paul is not referring to medical healing, but rather to a Spirit given ability to heal in the way that Jesus did. It is worth noting that in the Greek of the New Testament, Paul talks about the gift in the plural (1 Cor 12:10; 28; 29). The use of the plural can be interpreted in different ways. Firstly, it may be that Paul recognised that one person in the community might be able to heal one particular kind of sickness, e.g. bad backs, while others might be able to heal other ailments such as deafness, skin disease, depression etc. In that sense there would be different but complementary gifts of healing in the church. Secondly, Paul may have been referring to the fact that many people exercise the gift of healing, in that sense there is a gift of healings. Thirdly, Paul may have been suggesting that the gift of healing is ephemeral rather than permanent. As such, it is new each time it is exercised. There is reason to believe that this latter interpretation is the correct one. Unlike miracle working, healing is usually a process, one that is gradual. It often works in and through the remarkable recuperative abilities of the body's immune system at a faster rate than would be considered normal.

Some commentators are of the opinion that exorcism may be a dimension of the healing adverted to by St Paul.[38] In this connection it is worth recalling what St Peter said to Cornelius: 'God anointed Jesus of Nazareth with the Holy Spirit and power, and how he went around doing good and healing all who were under the power of the devil, because God was with him.' In this verse, healing and exorcism are virtually synonymous. Paul often spoke about the interrelated notions of spiritual warfare and deliverance. In Acts 16:16-19, Luke recounts how in Philippi, Paul's preaching was being interrupted by a young woman who was demonised. 'Finally Paul became so troubled that he turned around and said to the spirit, "In the name of Jesus Christ I command you to come out of her!" At that moment the spirit left her.' It could be argued, however, that rather than being a charism, exorcism is a sacramental. In par. 1673 of the CCC which deals with the subject of sacramentals we read, 'When the church asks publicly and authoritatively in the name

---

38. See footnote 69, Gordon D. Fee, *The First Epistle to the Corinthians*, 595.

of Jesus Christ that a person or object be protected against the power of the Evil One and withdrawn from his dominion, it is called exorcism.' Later, the same paragraph says, 'Before an exorcism is performed, it is important to ascertain that one is dealing with the presence of the Evil One, and not an illness.' So, although exorcism certainly demonstrates the power of God and is related to the charism of healings, it is separate and not properly speaking a *gratiae gratis datae*.

c) The gift of Working Miracles

When the Greek of 1 Cor 12:10 is literally translated into English it says, to some is given 'operations of works of power.' However most translators use the shorter phrase 'the working of miracles'. The word 'miracle' comes from the Latin *miraculum*, meaning 'a wonder'. From a religious point of view a miracle is a supernatural manifestation of divine power which goes beyond the laws of nature, as we currently understand them, in such a way as to evoke religious awe and wonder in those who witness it. The Catholic Church has stipulated that in order to declare that a healing is miraculous it must be established that the disease was serious; that there was objective proof of its existence; that other treatments had failed; and that the cure was rapid, lasting, and inexplicable from a scientific point of view.

We are told that some of the great heroes of faith in the Old Testament performed miracles. For instance Elijah raised a dead boy (2 Kgs 4:18-37), cured Naaman the leper (2 Kgs 5:1-19), multiplied food (2 Kgs 4:42-44) and had God consume his sacrifice with fire on Mount Carmel (1 Kgs 18:16-39). In the New Testament, Jesus was like a new Elijah,[39] who performed even greater miracles. He raised the dead (e.g. Jn 11:1-44), healed the sick (e.g. Mt 12:15), drove out demons (e.g. Mt 8:28-34), and performed nature miracles such as multiplying food (Mt 14:13-21), calmed a storm (Lk 8:22-25) and walked on water (Mt 14:25-27). Paul may have referred to nature miracles (cf Acts 16:26; 28:3f). Like Jesus, he and the other apostles performed marvellous

---

39. There is some justification for saying that Jesus was like a new Elijah because at his transfiguration he epitomised, surpassed and fulfilled all that was best in the law as represent by Moses, and in the prophets as represented by Elijah (Lk 9:28-36).

deeds, e.g. Peter raised Dorcas to life (Acts 9:40), Paul raised Eutychus (Acts 20:10) and in (Gal 3:5) the apostle speaks about the way God 'works miracles among you'.

CONCLUSION

This chapter intended to see if scripture would support the contention that the gifts of the Spirit mentioned in 1 Cor 12:8-10 could be legitimately classified as charisms of revelation, proclamation and demonstration. It seems fairly clear that the classification is justifiable. The remaining chapters of this book will argue that evangelisation, whether new or old, is made up of two main elements: revelation and expression. Expression of what is revealed can take two forms: a proclamation in words, and a demonstration in charismatic and non-charismatic deeds, such as healing and action for justice respectively. In chapter five we go on to describe the decline of charisms in the first millennium and their unexpected re-emergence at the end of the second.

CHAPTER THREE

St Thomas Aquinas on the evangelistic nature of the Gifts of the Spirit

St Thomas (1225-1274) lived in an age when the charismatic gifts were not much in evidence, except in the lives of saints, and so attention was mainly focused on those gifts of the Spirit which are mentioned in Is 11:2. Nevertheless, in a 'Treatise on the Gratuitous Graces,' in the *Summa Theologiae* II-II, q. 171-179 (hereafter, *ST*), St Thomas devoted more than 32,000 words to an examination of the charisms mentioned by St Paul, especially in 1 Cor 12:8-10. He also wrote about them in his *Commentary on the First Epistle to the Corinthians* (hereafter *FEC*), and in book 3, art. 155, of the *Summa Contra Gentiles* (hereafter *SCG*). There is also a relevant *Sermon and Collation of St Thomas Aquinas for the Feast of Pentecost* (hereafter *SCP*).[1] It is surprising to find that the teaching of the church's premier theologian on the gifts is by and large neglected. In this chapter an effort will be made to outline its main élan and content.

What were St Thomas's sources? Firstly, there were the scriptures which he had studied assiduously, as his many commentaries and the *Catena Aurea*[2] attest. Secondly, there were the lives of saints who had exercised the charisms. Presumably, Thomas was familiar the *Lives of the Brethren of the Order of Preachers 1206-1259* which describes how St Dominic de Guzman and Bl Jordan of Saxony exercised many of the charisms listed in 1 Cor 12:8-10, such as miracle working, healing the sick, and prophecy.[3] In view of the fact that they were contemporaries, it is quite possi-

---

1. This translation is based on the provisional critical edition of the Leonine Commission. Available at http://www4.desales.edu/~philtheo/loughlin/ATP/Sermons/Pentecost_Sermon.html (accessed on 26 March 2008).
2. A compilation of Patristic commentary on the four gospels. Cf Facsimile of 1841, 4 volume version trs John Henry Newman, (Tenby: Saint Austin Press, 1999).
3. Tran. Placid Conway OP, (London: Blackfriars Publications, 1955).

ble that St Thomas had read St Bonaventure's *The Life of Francis of Assisi*.[4] This remarkable book seems to have a simple thesis. The life of Jesus of Nazareth was reproduced, to a unique degree, in the founder of the Franciscans. The signs and wonders that Jesus performed on earth, Francis did in his name. Not only that, the *Povarello* bore the wounds of Jesus in his body. Thirdly, Thomas was familiar with the writings of the Fathers of the Church, including those that commented on 1 Cor 12:8-10. They seemed to propose two interrelated ways of looking at the charisms. For instance, reference was made in chapter two to St Cyril of Jerusalem's statement that instead of referring to doctrinal faith, the charism of faith, mentioned by Paul in 1 Cor 12:9, was about the kind of firm trust that moves mountains. However, it is clear that some Fathers of the Church, for instance Origen and Hillary of Poitiers, understood the charism of faith primarily in *didactic terms*. Others, such as St John Chrysostom and Bishop Eusebius of Caesarea, saw it primarily in *dynamic terms* as the key to deeds of power. What is true about the charism of faith could be extrapolated to apply to all the charisms. Mary Ann Fatula points out in her *Thomas Aquinas: Preacher and Friend*, that the Angelic Doctor was a contemplative, whose writings and preaching were rooted in his sustained attention to God in Christ.[5]

DID JESUS EXERCISE THE CHARISMS?

St Thomas espoused a high rather than a low Christology, in other words he tended to stress the divinity rather than the humanity of Christ. That being so it is not surprising to find that he believed that Jesus was charismatic. 'Christ,' he said, 'is the first and chief teacher of spiritual doctrine and faith, according to Hebrews 2:3, 4 ... Hence it is clear that *all the gratuitous graces were most excellently in Christ as in the first and chief teacher of the faith* [my italics].'[6] It is worth noting that in par. 4 of his encyclical *Divinum Illud Munus* (1897), on the Holy Spirit, Pope Leo XIII offered an authoritative endorsement of Thomas' view when he wrote: 'In him [Christ] ... were all the treasures of wisdom and

---

4. (Rockford, Il.: Tan Books, 1988).
5. (Collegeville: The Liturgical Press, 1993)
6. *ST* III, q. 7.

knowledge, graces *gratis datae*, [i.e. charisms] virtues, and all other gifts foretold in the prophecies of Isaias.' Thomas believed that through the indwelling of Christ in the heart through faith (cf Eph 3:14) by the powerful action of the Holy Spirit, Christians could seek to continue and fulfill all of Christ's earthly activities, including his charismatic activity.

A DIDACTIC, EVANGELISTIC UNDERSTANDING OF THE CHARISMS

Although St Thomas understood the charisms mainly in didactic terms, he also emphasised the role of deeds of power. In a way his approach was not surprising. It is interesting to note that the Dominican Constitutions stated: 'Our order was constituted principally for preaching and the salvation of souls.' In other words, the Dominicans were established to carry out the universal call to evangelise.[7] St Thomas referred to the role of the charisms in this enterprise when he wrote: 'The Holy Spirit provides sufficiently for the church in matters profitable unto salvation, to which purpose the gratuitous graces are directed.'[8]

It was suggested in the second chapter that the gifts of the Spirit could be classified in a threefold way, as revelatory, proclamatory, and demonstrative. A question arises: did St Thomas propose a classification of the gifts, and if so, was it similar or dissimilar to the one already proposed in chapter two? When one looks at his short description of the gratuitous gifts in the *SCG* and his much longer description in the *ST*, it is fairly obvious that he proposed a similar classification. For example, in the *SCG* he began by talking about revelation as 'an inner light of the mind'. He went on to say, 'Those who receive a revelation from God ought in the order of divine enactment to instruct others,'[9] i.e., by means of 'the grace of speech'. He then went on to say that what is proclaimed needs to be confirmed by deeds of power. He stated that the proof that the preacher's announce-

---

7. The Dominican mission statement was endorsed at the Second Vatican Council when it referred to the universal call to evangelise in par. 35 of the *Decree on the Missionary Activity of the Church*: 'The whole church is missionary, and the work of preaching the gospel is a fundamental duty of the People of God.'

8. *ST* II-I, q. 178, a. 1.

9. Book 3, par. 155.

ments came from God is, 'the evidence of works done by them such as none other than God could do, healing the sick, and other miracles.'[10] He said something very similar in the *ST*. Speaking about the gratuitous gifts of the Spirit he wrote succinctly, 'some of them pertain to knowledge [revelation], some to speech [proclamation], and some to operation [demonstration].'[11] He stated unequivocally that, 'all things pertaining to knowledge may be comprised under prophecy.' It is clear that St Thomas saw prophecy as the key to understanding the revelatory gifts and *ipso facto* all the charisms. In the *ST* he said: 'Now the prophet's mind is moved not only to apprehend something [i.e. Revelation], but also to speak [i.e. Proclamation] or to do something [i.e. Demonstration]; sometimes indeed to all these three together.'[12]

Later he said that Moses was the archetypal Old Testament prophet. Speaking about him, he observed: 'In prophecy we may consider not only the knowledge, whether by intellectual or by imaginary vision [revelation], but also the announcement [proclamation] and the confirmation by miracles [demonstration].'[13] It can be concluded, therefore, that although some scripture scholars may be skeptical about the threefold classification of charisms proposed in chapter two, St Thomas endorsed such a typology for scriptural and theological reasons.[14] In his time it had a strongly evangelistic dimension, especially in the form of kerygmatic preaching to non-believers and heretics such as the Moslems and Cathars, and also in the form of the catechesis of those who already had faith.

Before moving on, a number of general comments are appropriate. St Thomas examined the charisms in a section of the *ST* which deals with acts which only pertain to certain people, such as contemplatives, bishops or religious. All the baptised are called to live the Christian life and evangelise, but not all are

---

10. Bk 3, sec., 155.
11. *ST* II-II, into., q. 171.
12. *ST* II-II, q. 173, a. 4.
13. *ST* II-II, q. 174, a. 4, corpus.
14. See Enrique Dussel's comments on St Thomas's typology of the charisms, 'The Differentiation of Charisms', *Charisms in the Church: Concilium,* 109 (New York: The Seabury Press, 1978), 39.

called to participate in the same activities. As St Paul says: 'To one is given the gift …' (1 Cor 12:8).

Thomas considered the charisms to be gratuitous graces i.e. *gratiae gratis datae* which are granted for the sanctification of others. He said that gratuitous grace, 'is ordained to this, that a person may help another to be led to God.'[15] Speaking of sanctifying grace, i.e. *gratiae gratum facientes* he said it, 'ordains a man immediately to a union with his last end.'[16] In other words, sanctifying grace is given to help the recipient grow in holiness, whereas gratuitous grace is given in order to help others to grow in holiness. Echoing the constitutions of his order, St Thomas then went on to say that the sanctification of others is made possible by 'instructing them in divine things.' In par. 725 of *FEC*, and elsewhere, he added the surprising observation that it would be possible, though presumably unlikely, that a person in a state of mortal sin could be enabled to exercise a charism such as healing, for the up-building of another person. He explained, 'The Holy Spirit is manifested in two ways by graces of this sort. In one way as dwelling in the church by teaching and sanctifying it, as when a sinner, in whom the Holy Spirit does not dwell, works miracles to show that the faith of the church which he professes is true[17] … If they teach a true doctrine, sometimes they work true miracles as confirming their teaching, but not as an attestation of their holiness. Hence Augustine says that magicians work miracles in one way, good Christians in another, wicked Christians in another. Magicians by private compact with the demons, good Christians by their manifest righteousness, evil Christians by the outward signs of righteousness.'[18]

St Thomas also said that the charisms such as prophecy, healing, or miracle working were not permanent abilities. They are give afresh on each occasion that God sees fit.[19] At this point we move on to examine what charisms he assigned to each group, and the reasons he gave for doing so.

---

15. *ST* I-II, q. 111, a. 4, corpus; II-II, q. 117, a. 1; *SCG* chap. 154, trs Vernon J. Bourke, (New York: Image Books, 1956), 239ff.

16. *ST* I-II, q. 111, a. 5.

17. In *FEC* sec. 725.

18. *ST* II-II, q. 178, a..= 2, rep. obj. 3.

19. *SCG*, b. 3. a. 155; *ST* II-II, q. 171, a. 2.

GIFTS OF KNOWLEDGE / REVELATION

a) Prophecy & Rapture

As was mentioned above, St Thomas thought that all things pertaining to revealed knowledge could be gathered under prophecy.[20] It is quite evident from the number of words that he devoted to this subject that he thought it was very important. This section will not dwell on the detail of what Thomas said about the gift. Rather it will seek to show that, first and foremost, prophecy is about revealed knowledge even though, subsequently, it can find expression in speech. St Thomas defined this foundational gift as follows: 'Prophecy is a kind of knowledge impressed under the form of teaching on the prophet's intellect, by Divine revelation.'[21] The Angelic Doctor says that prophecy is not a form of natural knowledge which could be acquired by human effort. As a gratuitous gift, 'Prophetic knowledge is of things which naturally surpass human knowledge. Consequently we must say that prophecy strictly so called cannot be from nature, but only from Divine revelation.'[22]

Thomas has very interesting things to say in both *Summa*s about the way in which revelation is imparted to the human mind: 'This light, which inwardly enlightens the mind, [i.e the inner enlightenment and certainty that accompanies faith in the revealed truths of Christianity] is sometimes borne out by other aids to knowledge, both exterior and interior. They may be formed by divine power, some utterance, or locution, heard by the external senses. Or it may be an inner locution, caused by God, and perceived by fantasy [image]. Or there may be bodily appearances, external and visible, formed by God. Or such corporeal appearance [apparition] may be inwardly depicted in fantasy [e.g. a dream or vision]. By these means, aided by the light inwardly impressed on his mind, man receives a knowledge of divine things; whereas the inner light is sufficient of itself without them.'[23] In the *ST* there is a description of how

20. *ST* II-II, intro to q. 171.
21. *ST* II-II, q. 171, a. 6, corpus.
22. *ST* II-II, q. 172, a. 1, corpus.
23. *SCG*, b. 3. a. 155. For related material see Augustin Poulain SJ, 'Revelations and Visions,' *The Graces of Interior Prayer: A Treatise on Mystical Theology* (London: Keegan Paul, 1910), 299-399; Jordan

prophecies are received: 'The prophetic revelation takes place in four ways: namely, by the infusion of an intelligible light, by the infusion of intelligible species,[24] by impression or co-ordination of pictures in the imagination, and by the outward presentation of sensible images.'[25]

It seems fairly clear that St Thomas believed that prophetic knowledge could sometimes enable a person to foretell future events. In saying this he tended to contradict the view, mentioned in the foregoing chapter, that prophecy was more a question of forth-telling than fore-telling. He said: 'Revelation of future events belongs most properly to prophecy, and from this prophecy apparently takes its name.'[26] He seemed to be describing what modern day Pentecostals and Charismatics would refer to as the word of knowledge when he observed: 'It contains things pertaining to future events, according to Is 47:9.'[27] Although Thomas said that 'in prophetic revelation the prophet's mind is moved by the Holy Spirit,'[28] he believed that angels, who behold the vision of God, act as messengers or mediators between God and people. He said: 'The gratuitous graces are ascribed to the Holy Spirit as their first principle; yet

---

Aumann OP, 'Revelation,' *Spiritual Theology* (London: Sheed & Ward, 1982), 428-31; Harvey Egan SJ, 'Prophecy,' *Christian Mysticism: The Future of a Tradition* (New York: Pueblo, 1984), 321-22; Lisa Schwebel, *Apparitions, Healings and Weeping Madonnas: Christianity and the Paranormal* (New York: Paulist Press, 2004).

24. An insight which is derived from an image or phantasm.

25. *ST* II-II, q. 173, a. 3. Mention of intelligible species refers to concepts which are abstracted from sense experience (i.e. phantasms). This is a fundamental point in Thomistic epistemology. It was elucidated in *ST* I-I, q. 84, a. 7.

26. *ST* II-II, q. 171, a. 3.

27. See the quotations from Gordon Fee and David Pytches in the foregoing chapter, footnotes 27 and 28.

28. *ST* II-II, q. 173, a. 4. The belief that the angels mediated revelation can be traced back at least to *The Shepherd of Hermas* (c. 150 AD). In Commandment 11, on 'True and False Prophets,' the unknown author wrote: 'The angel of the prophetic spirit that is assigned to him fills the person, and being filled with the Holy Spirit the man speaks to the multitude just as the Lord wills.' *The Apostolic Fathers in English*, ed. Michael Holmes (Grand Rapids: Baker Academic, 2006), 237.

he works grace of this kind in men by means of the angels.'[29] In this connection he offered two warnings. Firstly, to be receptive to revelation requires that the mind be free to contemplate divine things. This ability 'is hindered by strong passions, and the inordinate pursuit of external things.'[30] Secondly, he warned that the Devil, as a fallen angel, can be the origin of a false prophecy: 'The revelation which is made by the demons,' he wrote, 'may be called prophecy in a restricted sense.'[31] It contains some truth in order to gain credibility for disguised lies. One is reminded in this regard of St Paul's belief that the Satan could appear as 'an angel of light' (2 Cor 11:14).

In the *ST* Thomas includes an interesting section on rapture states, which is closely related to the subject of prophecy. It is clear that what he had in mind was an experience of the kind described by St Paul in 2 Cor 12:2, where the apostle says 'He was caught up to the third heaven.'[32] Thomas says, 'Speaking of rapture, whereby a man is uplifted by the Spirit of God to things supernatural, and withdraws from his senses, according to Ezek 8:3, "The Spirit lifted me up between the earth and the heaven, and in visions of God he took me to Jerusalem".'[33] Commenting on such states Thomas said: 'Now revelation pertains to the intellective power. Therefore ecstasy or rapture does also.'[34] In other words, prophecy with cognitive content can be received when a person is in a state of religious rapture. It is possible that this kind of ecstasy is similar to that experienced by the pre-classical, and classical prophets of the Old Testament. It raises the question: Is the contemporary experience, which is variously referred to as 'slaying in the Spirit,' 'resting in the Spirit,' or 'the falling phenomenon,' sometimes an ecstatic state during which a prophetic revelation can be received? People in the Charismatic Movement do occasionally report having received

---

29. *ST* II-II, q. 172, a. 2, rep. obj., 2.
30. *ST* II-II, q. 172, a. 4.
31. *ST* II-II, q. 172, a. 5.
32. There is a very interesting and detailed observation on 2 Cor 12:1-4 in St Thomas's commentary on *The Second Epistle to the Corinthians*, trs Fabian Larcher, OP, pars. 440-65, http://www.aquinas.avemaria.edu/Aquinas-Corinthians-Sec2.pdf (accessed 2 April, 2008).
33. *ST* II-II, q. 175, a. 1.
34. *ST* II-II, q. 175, a. 2.

messages from the Lord while in that unusual state. In chapters 18-22 of her *Autobiography*, St Teresa of Avila says that the fourth stage of prayer is characteristically 'devotion of ecstasy or rapture'. In chapter twenty-one she wrote: 'In this state of ecstasy occur true revelations, great favours and visions, all of which are of service in humbling and strengthening the soul and helping it to despise the things of this life and to gain a clearer knowledge of the reward which the Lord has prepared for those who serve him.'[35]

It is hard to know which of these two kinds of rapture, resting in the Spirit, or mystical states typical of the fourth degree of prayer, that St Thomas had in mind. Arguably resting in the Spirit is merely an ecstatic state. But he says, 'Rapture adds something to ecstasy. For ecstasy simply means a going out of oneself by being placed outside one's proper order, whereas rapture denotes a certain violence in addition.'[36] What Teresa described is more in line with what Thomas said about rapture states and their revelatory component. What she described is also reminiscent of what Thomas said in *SCG* book 3, art. 155 about how revelation is received.

b) Discernment of Spirits
In view of the fact that St Thomas thought that the devil could reveal prophecies of a sort, it is important that the members of the Christian community have gifted members who are endowed with a God-given ability to distinguish prophecies that come from God from those that do not. In *FEC* he says, 'In regard to this Paul says: "To another [is given] the ability to distinguish between spirits," namely, in order that a man be able to discern by what spirit someone is moved to speak or work; for example, whether by the spirit of charity or by the spirit of envy.'[37] It would seem from this quotation that, unlike some contemporary scripture scholars,[38] St Thomas did not restrict

---

35. Translated & Edited by Allison Peers from the critical edition of Silverio De Santa Teresa, C. D.
36. *ST* II-II, q, 175, a. 2, reply obj. 2.
37. Sec., 728.
38. Cf Paul Kariuku Njiru, *Charisms and the Holy Spirit's Activity in the Body of Christ*, 161-165; Raymond F. Collins, *First Corinthians*, 455. However, there are other exegetes who agree with St Thomas's inter-

the charism of discernment of spirits to prophecy, but widened it to include the testing of any kind of inspiration or prompting.

A statement of St Thomas in the *SCG* can introduce this section. He said: 'Now because those who receive a revelation from God ought in the order of divine enactment to instruct others, there needed to be further communicated the grace of speech. Hence it is said: "The Sovereign Lord has given me an instructed tongue" (Is 50:4). "I will give you words and wisdom, which all your adversaries will not be able to resist or contradict" (Lk 21:15). Hence also the gift of tongues (Acts 2:4).'[39] Clearly, Thomas believed that the Lord gives people revealed knowledge not only to enlighten them personally, but also in order that they might enlighten others by means of verbal evangelisation. So, he examined the specific charisms, i.e. the gift of tongues, the interpretation of tongues, and the utterance of wisdom and knowledge which enable those who receive them to engage in effective evangelisation.

a) The Gift of Tongues
The previous chapter adverted to the fact that there are two main interpretations of the gift of tongues. Firstly, there is what is sometimes known as *xenoglossia*, i.e. an ability of a person to speak languages that he or she does not know. Some people think that this is the gift that enabled the apostles to communicate with the multinational crowd on Pentecost Sunday. St Thomas would probably have been familiar with the story of how on one occasion St Dominic and his companion Bertrand benefited from the hospitality and generosity of some German pilgrims. The two men prayed that they might be able to reciprocate by being able to talk about spiritual things and preach to them about Jesus Christ. Then, '... to the bewilderment of the pilgrims they began to speak fluently in German, and as they

---

pretation such as Gordon Fee, *The First Epistle to the Corinthians*, 596-597; George Montague, *The Holy Spirit: Growth of a Biblical Tradition*, 154-155.
39. Book 3, a. 155.

trudged along together during the next four days, they continued conversing about our Lord Jesus Christ until they came to Orleans.'[40]

Secondly, there is *glossolalia*, which according to Paul was a gift of unintelligible private prayer. As was noted in chapter two, it may also have acted as a form of pious utterance which required interpretation at meetings. Consistent with his didactic model of evangelisation, Thomas clearly interpreted the charism of tongues as *xenoglossi* in *ST* II-II q. 176 and in par. 729 of his *FEC*. He says that although Jesus did not exercise this gift because it was not necessary in Israel, he could have done so had it been necessary, because as God he knew all languages. Speaking about the apostles, he said that they were poor and powerless. They would have found it difficult to get interpreters to assist them in their work. Speaking of Peter he said that the gift of tongues was given, 'in order that he be able to speak in diverse languages, so that he would be understood by all, as it says of the apostles in Acts 2:4 that they spoke in various languages.'[41] He asks the question did the apostles speak one language which was understood by all, or did they speak the many languages of the people who were listening? It was the latter, he answered, because otherwise the gift would have 'amounted to an illusion, since a man's words would have had a different sound in another's ears, from that with which they were uttered.'[42]

It could be argued that Thomas's lack of personal experience of tongues and his theological *a priori* of a didactic kind led to a distorted understanding of the charism of tongues as described by Paul in 1 Cor 12:10 and elsewhere in chapter 14. Yes, *xenoglossi* was granted to the apostles on Pentecost Sunday, but surely Paul was speaking of *glossolalia* in 1 Cor 12:10 and in 1 Cor 13:8;

---

40. *Lives of the Brethren of the Order of Preachers 1206-1259*, Book II, sec. 10.
41. *FEC*, a. 155.
42. *ST* II-II, q. 176, a. 1, rep. obj. 2. It is a well attested fact that St Vincent Ferrer OP, had the gift of *xenoglossi*. In the course of the canonisation process it was juridically attested that although he spoke in his native Valencian, he was perfectly understood wherever he went, even though the people listening only understood their own native languages. See Andrew Pradel OP, *Angel of the Judgment: A Life of Vincent Ferrer* (Notre Dame, Indiana: Ave Maria Press, 1953), 137-38.

14:1-26. While Thomas seemed to appreciate, without adequate explanation, the fact that tongues can be a form of non-conceptual, non-imaginative prayer in *FEC* (pars. 838-39), he seemed to end up in an apparent contradiction in his commentary on 1 Cor 14:23-26. If speaking in tongues was *xenoglossi*, as it was on Pentecost, surely visitors to the Christian meetings would have understood what was being said in tongues without any need of an interpretation. As we shall see in the next chapter, Benedict XIV provided evidence from the lives of the saints which indicated that *xenoglossi* meant that the listeners who spoke many different languages understood the evangelist when he spoke in his own native tongue.

c) The Interpretation of Tongues

True to the orientation of the didactic model of evangelisation, St Thomas gives what seems to be a curious explanation of the charism of the interpretation of tongues. In par. 729 of *FEC* he says that it is a Spirit given ability to explain difficult scriptures. He quoted two texts, Dan 5:16 and Gen 40:8 in support of his view. His comments on 1 Cor 14:23 do not add any new insight. In a reply to an objection, he said in the *ST* that, 'The interpretation of speeches is reducible to the gift of prophecy, inasmuch as the mind is enlightened so as to understand and explain any obscurities of speech arising either from a difficulty in the things signified, or from the words uttered being unknown, or from the figures of speech employed, according to Dan 5:16, "I have heard that you are able to give interpretations and to solve difficult problems." Hence the interpretation of speeches is more excellent than the gift of tongues.'[43]

d) The Utterance of Wisdom and Knowledge

Given the fact that St Thomas was endowed, by God, with a remarkable gift of wisdom and knowledge, it is not surprising that he had insightful things to say about them in the *ST*. As Gerald Vann OP demonstrated in *The Divine Pity*, he correlated them with the virtues and the Beatitudes.[44] Thomas says succinctly,

43. *ST* II-II, q. 176, a. 2, rep. obj. 4.
44. (Notre Dame: Christian Classics, 1986).

'Knowledge of divine things is called wisdom, and all knowledge of human beings shares the more general term of knowledge.'[45] He says that wisdom is a kind of connatural awareness that is made possible by charity, which unites the knower to what is known. But in his commentary on the *FEC*, par. 727, he explains: 'It is significant that the apostle places in the charismatic graces not wisdom and knowledge, but the utterance of wisdom and knowledge, which pertain to the ability to persuade others by speech about matters pertaining to wisdom and knowledge.'

In his commentary on the *FEC*, par. 727, having said that wisdom is knowledge of divine things, he went on to say that by means of the utterance of wisdom, the graced person 'can persuade one in things pertaining to the knowledge of divine things.' In the commentary on the *FEC* he says that the utterance of knowledge is an ability to manifest the things of God through creatures. Thomas says that the gifts of utterance become effective in three ways: by instructing the intellect, moving the person emotionally, and swaying the hearers to a love of what has been spoken of in words. Speaking of women he said that they can exercise the gifts of the utterance of wisdom and knowledge in private, domestic situations, but not in public.[46] Not only is the Spirit at work in the one who speaks, he is also at work in the one who hears. 'Hence Gregory says in a homily for Pentecost (Hom. XXX, in Ev.): "Unless the Holy Ghost fill the hearts of the hearers, in vain does the voice of the teacher resound in the ears of the body".'[47]

GIFTS OF DEMONSTRATION

Through the prophetic gifts of revelation, a person gets to know the truths of faith. Through the gifts of proclamation, such as the ability to speak foreign languages and to communicate wisdom and knowledge, revelation is imparted to others. But St Thomas says that the trans-rational truth of what is said needs to be confirmed by the working of deeds of power. In the *SCG* he stated

---

45. *ST* II-II, q. 9, a 2, corpus.
46. *ST* II-II, q. 177, a. 2.
47. *ST* II-II, q. 177, a. 1.

this clearly, 'Any announcement put forth requires confirmation before it can be received – unless indeed it is self-evident, and the truths of faith are not evident to human reason – there was need of something to confirm the announcements of the preachers of the faith. But, inasmuch as they transcend reason, they could not be confirmed by any demonstrative process of reasoning from first principles. The means, therefore, to show that the announcements of these preachers come from God was the evidence of works done by them such as none other than God could do, healing the sick, and other miracles.'[48] In 1 Cor 12:9-10 St Paul refers to three charisms of power: the kind of faith that can move mountains, and gifts of healing; and miracle working. St Thomas had very interesting things to say about each one of them as will be seen.

a) The Charism of Faith

It would appear that Thomas understood the charism of faith in two different, but complementary ways. Firstly, in his treatise on grace in *ST* II-I, he interprets the gift in a didactic manner: 'Enumerated here under the gratuitous graces, not as a virtue justifying man himself, but *as implying a super-eminent certitude of faith*, whereby a person is fitted for instructing others concerning such things as belong to the faith.'[49]

Secondly, in his biblical commentary on 1 Cor 12:9 Thomas referred to the special didactic gift, but proceeded to describe the charism of faith as a necessary prerequisite for miracle working. In an article entitled 'Whether there is a gratuitous grace of working miracles?' he says: 'The working of miracles results from faith – either of the worker, according to 1 Cor 13:2, "If I should have all faith, so as I could move mountains," or of other persons for whose sake miracles are wrought, according to Mt 13:58, "And he wrought not many miracles there, because of their unbelief." Therefore, if faith be reckoned a gratuitous grace, it is superfluous to reckon in addition the working of signs as another gratuitous grace.'[50]

A little later, he added: 'The working of miracles is ascribed

---

48. Book 3. a. 155.
49. *ST* , I-II, q. 111, a. 4, reply obj. 2.
50. *ST* II-II, q. 178, a.1., obj. 5.

to faith for two reasons. First, because it is directed to the confirmation of faith; secondly, because it proceeds from God's omnipotence on which faith relies. Nevertheless, just as besides the grace of faith, the grace of the word is necessary that people may be instructed in the faith, so too is the grace of miracles necessary that people may be confirmed in their faith.'[51]

b) Healings and Miracle Working

Understood in this second way, St Thomas saw the charism of faith as the gift whereby healings and miracles could be performed. He saw these two gifts like two sides of the same coin of the miraculous. In par. 728 of his commentary on *FEC*, Thomas clearly stated that there are two kinds of deeds of power, namely healings and the working of miracles. Speaking of miracles he said that 'The things God does when he bypasses the causes we know about, we call miracles.'[52] He described the distinction between healings and miraculous deeds as follows: 'The grace of healing is mentioned separately [from that of miracles] because by its means a benefit, namely bodily health, is conferred on man in addition to the common benefit bestowed in all miracles, namely the bringing of men to the knowledge of God.'[53]

Many medieval saints such as Dominic Guzman, Anthony of Padua and Francis of Assisi were renowned for their healing deeds. In his commentary on 1 Cor 12:9, in *FEC* he simply says that that healing is simply ending someone's infirmity. Commenting on miracle working Thomas said that, 'Two things may be considered in miracles. One is that which is done: this is something surpassing the faculty of nature, and in this respect miracles are called virtues. The other thing is the purpose for which miracles are wrought, namely the manifestation of something supernatural, and in this respect they are commonly called signs, but on account of some excellence they receive the name of wonder or prodigy, as showing something from afar.'[54] In his commentary on the *FEC* he gives examples of what he means, when he instances two Old Testament nature miracles, the di-

---

51. *ST* II-II, q. 178, a. 1.
52. *ST* 1-1, q. 105, a. 8, corpus.
53. *ST* II-II, q. 178, a. 1, rep. obj. 4.
54. *ST* II-II, q. 178, a.1.

viding of the sea (Ex 14:21) and the standing still of the sun and moon in the heavens (Jos 10:13).

CONCLUSION

Given the fact that St Thomas lived in an age when the charisms were not widely exercised, his description of the gifts of the Spirit is not only surprising in its detail, it is a *tour de force* as far as its depth and coherence are concerned. His 32,000 word essay still has a great contribution to make in the contemporary church where, by the grace of God, the charisms are being exercised by so many people around the world. What makes St Thomas's views so interesting in terms of this book, is the fact that he interpreted them within a didactic model of evangelisation. He classified the gifts of the Spirit under the headings of revelation, proclamation and demonstration. He showed how evangelisation begins in prophetic revelation which finds expression in teaching and preaching. Scripture underlines the importance of leading people to believe in the good news by means of inspired proclamation. It says in Rom 10:14-17, 'How could they [the unbelievers] have faith in him [Christ] without having heard of him? And how could they hear without someone to spread the news? And how could anyone spread the news without being sent? ... So then faith comes from hearing, and hearing through the word of Christ.' Nowadays we need anointed homilists who only preach what God has revealed to them in prayer. We also need committed catechists and religion teachers, whether in the classroom or the home, who only impart what they themselves personally know and believe.

As was noted in chapter one, verbal witness needs to find expression in a life well lived. In this regard the church has always stressed the importance of compassion. St Thomas wrote: 'Compassion is heartfelt identification with another's distress, driving us to do what we do to help ... As far as outward activity is concerned, compassion is the Christian's whole rule of life.'[55] Compassion can take the form of corporal and spiritual works of mercy, especially generosity to the poor. It also emphasises the importance of identifying the unjust and oppressive causes of

---

55. St Thomas wrote in *ST* II-II, q. 30, a. 1 corpus.

poverty and working to change them by means of appropriate political and social action.

Needless to say, St Thomas would have agreed with these points, but what makes his treatise on the charisms so relevant is his emphasis on the vital role of signs and wonders in effective evangelisation. In 1979, Francis McNutt gave memorable expression to this point in an article entitled 'What God Has Joined Together,' which was about the complementary relationship between the charismatic and the institutional elements in the church: 'A gift of preaching,' he wrote, 'is strengthened by other manifestations of the power of the Holy Spirit. St Paul states that in his sermons he did not depend on arguments that belonged to philosophy but on a "demonstration of the Spirit and power" (1 Cor 2:4). St Thomas Aquinas, in his commentary on this passage, states that the preacher of the gospel should preach as Jesus did, confirming the message either through healings and miracles or by living such a holy life that can only be explained by the power of the Spirit. If I preach the power of Jesus Christ to save and redeem the whole person, people want to see that power made real. They want to see the saving, freeing power of Jesus when we pray that the spiritually sick be given the power to repent, and that the emotionally and physically sick be healed, and may be made better as a sign that the message of salvation and healing are true.'[56]

---

56. *New Covenant* (March, 1979), 13.

CHAPTER FOUR

Benedict XIV on the link between the charisms, holiness and evangelisation

Prospero Lambertini was born in Bologna in 1675. By the age of 19 he had received a doctorate in theology and canon law. While St Thomas Aquinas was his favourite author, he was so widely read that he was reputed to be one of the most erudite men of his time. He lived in the Age of Enlightenment when the church was being attacked by rationalist philosophers and challenged by absolutist rulers. In 1712 he was appointed canon theologian at the Vatican and assessor of the Congregation of Rites. In 1731 he became archbishop of his native city. Later in 1740 he was elected Pope following a consistory which lasted six months. He took the name of Benedict XIV. It has been said that he was possibly the most learned Pope to have ever graced the chair of Peter. He died in 1758 at the age of 83.[1]

While he was at the Congregation of Rites, Lambertini had the responsibility of assessing the causes of people who had been put forward for possible beatification and canonisation. It raised the question in the bishop's mind, what criteria should be used? Eventually, he wrote a massive work entitled *On the Beatification and Canonization of the Servants of God*. In 1850, the English Oratorians translated part of the Latin version into English. They published three volumes under the general title *Heroic Virtue* (hereafter *HV*), the third of which dealt with the charisms at considerable length.[2] Next to Thomas's treatment of the same subject in the *Summa Theologica*, it is the longest study of the charisms in 1 Cor 12:8-10 by an authoritative Catholic author up to the twentieth century. It would have to be said, how-

---

1. I'm aware of only one biography of Benedict XIV in English. Renee Haynes, *Philosopher King: The Humanist Pope Benedict XIV* (London: Weidenfeld & Nicolson, 1970).
2. Prospero Lambertini, *Heroic Virtue: Treatise on the Beatification and Canonization of the Servants of God*, vol. 3, (New York: Duignan & Brother, 1851), 88-230.

ever, that whereas Thomas's treatise on the charisms in 1 Cor 12:8-10 is a *tour de force* of originality and theological coherence, Lambertini's well informed treatise, though interesting and useful, is derivative. It depends largely on Thomas and those theologians who commented on his thought. Whereas Thomas looked at the charisms in the light of the church's universal call to evangelise,[3] Prospero Lambertini, looked at them in the light of the church's universal call to holiness, a call that was well expressed in par. 39 of the *Constitution of the Church*, of the Second Vatican Council: 'In the church, everyone whether belonging to the hierarchy, or being cared for by it, is called to holiness, according to the saying of the apostle: "For this is the will of God, your sanctification".'

The lives of some of the great saints such as Anthony of the Desert, Benedict, and Francis of Assisi, show that there was an intimate connection between the witness of their personal holiness and their evangelisation which often involved charismatic activity.[4] Not surprisingly, the church has always affirmed the connection between holiness of life and evangelisation. For instance in par. 76 of *EN*, Paul VI wrote: 'Our evangelising zeal must spring from true holiness of life, and as the Second Vatican Council suggests, preaching must in its turn make the preacher grow in holiness, which is nourished by prayer and above all by love for the Eucharist.' In *RM* par. 90 John Paul II wrote: 'A missionary is really such only if he commits himself to the way of holiness: Holiness must be called a fundamental presupposition and an irreplaceable condition for everyone in fulfilling the mission of salvation in the church.'

CHARISMS AS POSSIBLE SIGNS OF HOLINESS

Toward the end of his reflections on the charisms, St Thomas said that miracles can be worked by God for two reasons. Firstly, as was noted in the preceding chapter, the charisms, especially of power, are granted for the sanctification of others. Their exercise in the name of Jesus does not necessarily imply the sanctity

---

3. Par. 35 of the *Decree on the Missionary Activity of the Church*.
4. Popes Paul VI and John Paul II repeatedly talked about the importance of being credible witness to the gospel. Cf *Evangelii Nuntiandi* pars. 21; 26; 41; 76 and *Redemptoris Missio*, par. 42.

of the one through whom the miracle was performed. Indeed that person could him or herself be in the state of mortal sin.[5] Secondly, Thomas went on to add: 'In the second way miracles are not wrought except by the saints, since it is a proof of their holiness that miracles are wrought during their lifetime or after death, either by themselves or by others.'[6]

Surely, this Thomistic distinction raises a problem for anyone who is assessing the life of a reputed saint. Do miracles, or, for that matter, charismatic activity of any kind, necessarily indicate that the person has reached the level of heroic sanctity? Lambertini himself adverted to this question in his book. He asked whether any account should be taken of gifts *gratis datae*? If they were absent in a person's life, should that fact act as an impediment to the advance of his or her cause?[7] In order to answer his question, the future Pope quoted the Fathers of Salamanca, as he often did, with approval: 'Because it cannot be denied that virtues greatly dispose towards, and assist the bestowal of the aforesaid graces, they are, therefore, for the most part given, not to sinners, but to the just: and in the canonisation of saints stand in the next place after the virtues.'[8] So the bishop concluded that if there was evidence of heroic virtue in a person's life, then and only then, were the graces *gratis datae* an indication of saintliness. Because this book is about the role of the charisms of revelation, proclamation, and demonstration in the new evangelisation, not much space will be devoted to this point.[9] However, it illustrates how the bishop's purpose was different from that of St Thomas. Whereas the Angelic Doctor interpreted the charisms within a context of active evangelisation, Lambertini was mainly interested in them as a possible sign of sanctity.

HIS APPROACH TO THE CHARISMS

Although it is quite evident that he had closely read what St Thomas had written about the charisms, Lambertini made no

5. *ST* II-II, q. 172, a. 4.
6. *ST* II-II, q. 178. a. 2.
7. Lambertini, *Heroic Virtue*, vol 3, 92.
8. Ibid., p. 94.
9. Suffice it to say that he thought that proof of great virtue and the fruits of the Spirit were the really important points to consider.

explicit effort to classify them into different groupings as his mentor had done. It can be noted in passing that he did briefly advert to Thomas's classification in chapter eight where he said: 'In prophetic revelation the mind is moved by the Holy Ghost, and moved to apprehend something [i.e. revelation], to speak something [i.e. proclamation] and to do something [i.e. demonstration].'[10] In spite of noting this classification, Lambertini did not utilise it, in any clear way, in his own treatment of the gifts. However, it does show that he did endorse Thomas's classification but did not utilise it because his purpose in writing was different from that of his theological mentor. As we shall see below, the order in which he studied the gifts was the same as the sequence put forward by St Paul. It could be said in a generalised way that any Christian who led an exceptionally holy life, would *ipso facto* have carried out the great commission. Given that demonstration in deeds is an essential aspect of evangelisation, saints are exceptional witnesses to God's loving presence, whether by their loving relationships and works of mercy, or by their charismatic activities. In volume three of *HV* Bishop Lambertini did make comments in passing which threw light on the evangelising role of those charisms in the lives of the saints and blesseds. For example, he stressed on many occasions that the charisms mentioned in 1 Cor 12:8-10 were 'manifestations'. As such they were not given for private use, but rather for the edification of the church, 'making manifest by some outward sign that the Holy Spirit is working by it.'[11] In general terms, such up-building of the faith and holiness of people is a form of evangelisation if for no other reason than that it witnesses to the presence and power of the risen Lord. From this point onwards, we will survey what the future Pope had to say about each of the gifts *gratis datae*.

WISDOM AND KNOWLEDGE

Lambertini began by acknowledging that in 1 Cor 12:8 St Paul was not referring to the first two of the seven gifts of the Holy Spirit, which are graces *gratum faciens*. Like St Thomas before

---

10. *Heroic Virtue*, vol 3, 198.
11. Ibid., 90-91.

him, he pointed to the fact that the apostle was referring to the special gifts *gratis datae*, of utterances of wisdom and knowledge. Typical of his erudite style, he went on to quote the opinions of a number of notable writers such as Augustine, Jerome, Thomas Aquinas, and Bishop Theodoret of Cyrus on the nature of the two gifts. Then he added his own description: 'The word of wisdom, then, is the external word of Divine things; by which a man without human study and labour, so discourses of Divine mysteries as to make it manifest that the Holy Ghost speaks in him, and none may gainsay him, by whom unbelievers are converted to, and the faithful confirmed in, the faith. And the word of knowledge is nothing else but discourse or speech on moral matters, relating to everlasting salvation, going forth readily without human study and labour, in writing or by word of mouth, where by those who hear it, understand that it proceeds not from human power, but Divine.'[12] It is worth noting how Lambertini acknowledged that these gifts have an evangelistic dimension insofar as they can be instrumental in the conversion of unbelievers. Having defined how the gifts involve revealed knowledge, he gave examples of men such as Sts Vincent Ferrer, Louis Bertrand, and Nicholas Fattore, together with women such as Judith and Esther in the Old Testament and Teresa of Avila in the sixteenth century, who could effect remarkable changes in their listeners, either publicly or privately, by the power of their anointed words. For instance, at Mount St Martha, Louis Bertrand baptised 15,000 Indians who had been converted to the faith as a result of his preaching.

Lambertini then went on to ask how the people, who were gifted with these two charisms of proclamation, got their wisdom and knowledge. He suggested that it was acquired by a combination of study, and in some people, e.g. Sts Thomas Aquinas, Teresa of Avila, Ignatius of Loyola, and Didacus Ximenes, it was also infused by God through the action of the Holy Spirit. Indeed he quotes something St Thomas said about this point: 'God made man capable of acquiring wisdom and knowledge by natural abilities and study and, therefore, when a man attains to wisdom and knowledge in another way than this,

12. Ibid., 103-4.

it is miraculous.'[13] This whole section is reminiscent of St Thomas's comments on the prophetic type of revelation that informs the proclamation of the evangelisers although, surprisingly, Lambertini does not refer to that fact. One would suspect that for a man who was so learned, this omission was deliberate rather than inadvertent.

FAITH, HEALING AND MIRACLES

a) The Charism of Faith

There may be a little confusion in the learned bishop's treatment of the charism of faith. In chapter four of *Heroic Virtue*, where he dealt with the charisms of the utterance of wisdom and knowledge, he quoted, with apparent approval, from a writer called Epagomene Viguier who referred not only to the utterance of wisdom and knowledge, but also to the 'utterance of faith'.[14] It should be said that there is no justification for this translation of the Greek of 1 Cor 12:9. It makes no mention of a 'message' or 'utterance' of faith. It is quite likely that Lambertini was following St Thomas at this point. He referred to the latter's didactic interpretation. Having admitted that this understanding of faith sounded like a grace *gratum faciens*, he asked how it could be a gift *gratis datae*? He answered by referring back to St Thomas, who had said quite clearly that while justifying faith is a grace *gratum faciens*, there is another kind of faith which is a gift *gratis datae* insofar as 'it imparts a *certain pre-eminent certainty of faith* [my italics], by which a man becomes capable of teaching others those things which belong to faith.'[15] He instanced two situations where this gift could be operative: witnessing to one's faith before a tyrant, or proposing it as a higher way to others, presumably unbelievers.

Having dealt with faith from the didactic point of view, the bishop went on, as St Thomas had done before him, to consider the charism of faith as the pre-requisite for the charisms of healing and miracle working, i.e. the faith to move mountains (1 Cor 13:2). In this particular chapter of his book, he refers to the teaching of so many saints and scholars that it is hard to know how he

---

13. Idid., 113.
14. Ibid., 103.
15. ST II-I, q. 111, a. 4, reply obj. 2.

himself understood the charism. He omitted any definition of his own. He considered five ways in which Francisco Suarez had examined the charism of faith and agreed with the Jesuit's belief that it was a grace *gratis datae* in virtue of which miracles and healings were performed by people as a result of their firm confidence in God. He then went on to quote John Chrysostom and Theodoret of Cyrus in support of this view. The former made a distinction between doctrinal faith and the faith to perform miracles; while the latter said that St Paul was not referring to ordinary saving faith, but rather to the faith that does admirable miracles which 'thereby bring men to the truth.'[16] Lambertini added by way of comment, 'According to this explanation, the grace of faith is nearly identical with the grace of healing and miracle working.'[17] He asked, as Thomas had already done, if faith was the key to healings and miracle working, in what sense could it be said that they were separate gifts *gratis datae*? He offered Thomas's answer, namely, that the healings or miracles are performed by the power of God and confirm what the person of faith has proclaimed. In that sense they are separate. Clearly, Bishop Lambertini, agreed that the charisms of demonstration, confirm what has been shared by means of the charisms of proclamation, although he did not use that exact terminology.

b) The Charisms of Healings and Miracle Working
The future Benedict XIV also considered the question which had already been asked and answered by St Thomas in the *ST*, namely, how does the charism of healings differ from that of miracle working? Having quoted from the fathers of Salamanca who talked generically of miracles which could take the form of healing, or some other form such as the changing of water into wine, he went on to quote St Thomas with approval: 'The grace of healing is mentioned separately, because thereby some benefit is conferred upon man, namely, of bodily health, over and above the general benefit which is shown in all miracles, namely,

---

16. Lambertini, *Heroic Virtue*, 127-128.
17. Ibid., 128.
18. Ibid., 129. Neither Thomas nor Lambertini make the point that, whereas healings are usually gradual, to a greater or lesser extent, miracles are instantaneous. It could also be said that, whereas the charism of

that men may be led to the knowledge of God.'[18]

Lambertini went on to make a succession of points that are worth noting. Firstly, he did not think that either the charisms of healings or miracle working were a permanent endowment. He felt that they were given afresh by God on each occasion they were exercised. Secondly, although he thought that healings and miracles were abundant in the early church in order to demonstrate the truth of the apostolic teaching, he did not entirely subscribe to the cessationist theory. Like St Augustine, he believed that healings and miracles continued to be experienced in the church as a result of trust in the sacraments, use of holy relics, and the prayers and ministry of saints. In spite of the fact that he believed that sinful people could be granted the gift of healings and miracle working, he did not say anything about ordinary lay people exercising them. They seemed to be the reserve of the saints whose causes he investigated. That anomaly, it should be noted, was a characteristic of all those who wrote about the gifts *gratis datae*, including St Thomas. In view of the fact that the charisms were demonstrably useful for the edification of the church and effective evangelisation, especially among unbelievers, they did not satisfactorily answer the question, why can ordinary Christians no longer exercise them as they once did in the early Church? Thirdly, Lambertini, believed with St Thomas, that whenever healings or miracles were performed, they were a confirmation of the faith recently preached.

Although Bishop Lambertini did not deal with exorcism under the heading of healings or miracles, he included a thorough discussion of the subject entitled, *'De ejectione Daemonum a corporibus obsessis,'* in volume four of his *opus* which is only available in Latin.[19] It deals with true and pseudo forms of possession and how to deal with them. The Cardinal did not relate exorcism with the charisms, or for that matter with evangelis-

---

healing tends to empower and accelerate the natural healing powers of the body's immune system, e.g. recovery from cancer, miracles go beyond the laws of nature as we understand them, e.g. immediate and permanent recovery from an incurable illness such as motor neuron disease. Admittedly, this perspective is a modern, scientific one which may not have been current at the time.

19. Prosperi Cardinalis de Lambertinis, *De Servorum Dei Beatificatione, et beatorum Canonizatione*, vol 4. (Rome: Prati, 1841), 325-336.

ation, but rather he looked at it as a feature in the lives of some of the saints, e.g. he quotes a story from the life of St Bernard by Gaufrido Monacho Claraevallensi, to do with a young man who was demonised.[20]

PROPHECY

Just as St Thomas had devoted a lot of space to the charism of prophecy in the *ST*, Prospero Lambertini devoted no fewer than seventy-six pages of his book to the same gift. Although he repeatedly quoted St Thomas, for some strange reason he failed to emphasise the important theological fact that his mentor believed that prophecy was the key to a sequential dynamic, i.e. receiving revealed knowledge, proclaiming the good news, and proving the divine origin of both by means of healings and miracles. He did say that 'prophecy consists in knowledge, and in the manifestation of what is known'[21] without expanding the point in an obviously evangelical way. Lambertini did proffer two descriptions of prophecy, the shorter of which said: 'A prophet, then, is he who foretells future events, or reveals to others things past, or present things hidden; although generally, and for the most part, prophecy is confined to the foretelling of future events.'[22]

The notion of foretelling future events is self-explanatory. Lambertini referred to 1 Pet 1:10 in support of this point. Prophecy can refer to past events. By way of example he referred to the manner in which Jesus knew that the Samaritan woman at the well had lived with a number of men. A prophecy can be about the present. For instance, Jesus knew what Simon the Pharisee was thinking when Mary washed his feet with tears. The second and third of these forms of prophecy sound like the ability to read hearts, which might be considered to be forms of the word of knowledge. Lambertini's treatment of prophecy is not particularly original. He tends to reiterate many of St Thomas's points of view while quoting authorities of his day who had commented on Thomas's writings. For example, he says that although prophecies are inspired by God, they are

20. Ibid., 334-35.
21. Lambertini, *Heroic Virtue*, vol 3, 139.
22. Ibid., 137.

often made possible by the mediation of angels.[23] He also stayed close to Thomas's description of the three ways in which a prophet can receive revealed knowledge: firstly, by means of the exterior senses, secondly, by means of the inner senses, and thirdly, by means of intellectual representations. Lambertini observed that these means of revelation should not be strictly divided because they can often overlap.[24] He also said that, although it is preferable that a prophet lead a good moral life, it is not strictly speaking necessary because the gift of prophecy is a *gratis datae*.[25] That said, he did observe, 'It is necessary for prophesying that the mind should be raised to the highest contemplation of spiritual things; this may be prevented through violent passions and inordinate attention to outward things.'[26]

Quoting a certain Cardinal Giovanni de Bona, he said in chapter six of *Heroic Virtue*, Book 3, that 'for the most part, this gift is bestowed by God upon holy men.'[27] He added that in causes of canonisation and beatification, prophetic activity of any kind should not be taken into account unless and until it had been established that the person had led a life of eminent holiness and virtue. He cited the example of many saints, such as Columbanus, Pius V, Teresa of Avila, Philip Neri, Mary Magdalene de Pazzi, Louis Bertrand, Paschal Baylon, Margaret of Cortona, Rose of Lima, Peter of Alcantara, Francesca Romana, and Francis Xavier, all of whom exercised the gift of prophecy in their lifetimes. They did so, for instance, by knowing contemporaneous events which were happening at a distance; by foretelling future events, e.g. their own and other people's deaths, and by reading people's hearts in such a way that they knew their state of conscience and their secret sins. Lambertini asked whether a person could have a permanent gift of prophecy. He answered by saying that only Christ had this capacity. Speaking in terms of a high Christology, he said that Jesus, 'In virtue of the hypostatic union, had, in this life, blessed and infused knowl-

23. Ibid., 142-45. This point of view is derived from S. Dionysius's *Heavenly Hierarchy* which espouses a rather Platonic worldview.
24. Ibid.,. 141-142.
25. Ibid., 149; 153.
26. Ibid., 155.
27. Ibid., 191.

edge, whereby he knew all truths which can be revealed by prophecy to men and so could, of his own proper and habitual or abiding knowledge, prophecy, without waiting for any revelation or the word of God.'[28] For Christians, the prophetic gift comes and goes as God wills. Lambertini also observed that when a person utters a prophecy, he or she may believe it is from God, while in reality it originated in the human spirit.

Lambertini devoted a chapter to asking interesting questions such as, is there a natural kind of prophecy? and can the devil inspire a prophecy? His approach was philosophical and theological rather than para-psychological or scientific. With regard to the first question, he stated that 'philosophers teach correctly that there is no faculty of knowing future events implanted in the human soul.'[29] That would seem to rule out any kind of psychic ability, such as clairvoyance, that would enable one to attune to events which transcended the normal laws of efficient causality. They have been written about by people such as Jung, who described synchronicity, John Bell, who suggested there was a form of non-local causality, and David Bohm, who theorised about an implicit as opposed to an explicit order in the universe.[30] Lambertini adverted to, and rejected, the Platonic notion that knowledge does not always have to begin in the senses. The idealist Greek philosopher believed that ideas were prior to created reality and postulated that a person could be in touch with those ideas, e.g. about the future, without the aid of the senses. Plato also believed that humans had a prior existence in the transcendent realm of pure ideas. In a sense their lives on earth are like those of recovering amnesiacs who remember what they already knew. Clearly, like St Thomas before him, Lambertini adopted a realistic Aristotelian approach. Only God can know all things in their ultimate nature and causes. As a result, neither angel nor devil can know future events with certainty. He did

28. Ibid., 158. It is hard to reconcile this observation with what Jesus said himself: 'I do nothing on my own but speak just what the Father has taught me' (Jn 8:28).
29. Ibid., 173.
30. Cf Pat Collins, 'ESP and Inspired Words of Knowledge,' in *Mind and Spirit: Spirituality and Psychology in Dialogue* (Dublin: Columba, 2006), 91-112.

allow for the fact that good and bad spirits, and to a lesser extent people, could predict rather than prophecy future events with a greater or lesser degree of probability. They could do this on the basis of their knowledge of the workings of the world and its necessary causes. He made the interesting and significant point that while the evil one knows what people do, he does not know what they think. That is known only to God. That said, using what information he has, the devil can inspire a pseudo-prophecy which might mimic the real thing in an impressive, but ultimately deceptive way. This possibility raises the whole issue of discerning whether prophecies are truly from God or not.

Having quoted the well known verse: 'Do not put out the Spirit's fire, do not treat prophecies with contempt. Test everything. Hold on to the good' (1 Thess 5:19), Lambertini went on to suggest three main criteria that could be used in the assessment of prophecies. It is worth noting that he did this in a chapter devoted to prophecy, rather than in the following chapter, which is devoted, among other things, to the charism of discernment of spirits. He said that the first criterion to use in distinguishing true from false prophecy is this: was it in accord with the teachings of Jesus, the apostles, and church law?[31] Following that, the question has to be asked, was the prophecy beyond human knowledge? Writing about this point the bishop said that it had to be asked, 'Whether he who foretold them [future events] could have had any conjectural knowledge thereof from signs, guesses, or experience. Again, whether he revealed the future hesitatingly, using such words as 'per chance,' 'perhaps,' 'it may be,' whether also in revealing and foretelling, he made use of human reasons in proof of what he said or, in doing this, whether he was subject to any human affection as, for instance, the hope, or the possible hope, of temporal advantage, or to mental agitation and, lastly, whether he truly knew, if not all, at least, some of those things of which he prophesied. All these questions must be very minutely investigated before it can be pronounced to have been real prophecy.'[32]

The second point to be taken into account, when assessing a

---

31. Lambertini, *Heroic Virtue*, vol 3, 193, 194.
32. Ibid., 194.

prophecy, is the interior state of the prophet. Although he did not put the point in Ignatian terms, Lambertini asked whether the person who spoke was in a state of inner desolation or consolation, because only those who manifest the interior fruits of the Spirit such as joy and peace (Gal 5:22-23), are to be trusted. He quoted St John Chrysostom and Cardinal Giovanni de Bona in support of his point. The latter said that false prophets speak when their minds are disturbed, because they cannot endure the assaults of the devil, who influences them. But he added: 'They whom God moves, speak with gentleness, humility and modesty.'[33] Finally, there is a third and decisive criterion: were the prophet's words fulfilled? He quoted Deut 18:21 in support of his point. It reads: 'How can we know when a message has been spoken by the Lord? If what a prophet proclaims in the name of the Lord does not take place or come true, that is a message that has not been spoken.' Lambertini added two caveats to this criterion. He saw that it was quite conceivable that a person would get a genuine prophetic word from the Lord, but would misinterpret its meaning. It was also possible that the Lord could warn people by means of a threat of future disaster. However, it might not take place, not because the prophecy was false, but because the people to whom it was addressed, repented, thereby averting God's wrath. Jonah's revoked prophecy against Nineveh would be an Old Testament example. Whereas St Thomas dealt with rapture states immediately after his examination of prophecy, Bishop Lambertini dealt with topics such as ecstasies, raptures, visions, and apparitions after his examination of the charisms in 1 Cor 12:8-10.[34]

DISCERNING OF SPIRITS, TONGUES AND INTERPRETATION OF TONGUES

a) The Charism of the Discernment of Spirits

Lambertini suggested that there were two ways in which reference to discernment of spirits could be understood. Firstly, there is the art of discernment of spirits which can be conducted in accordance with the rules set forth by ascetics, mystics and contemplative theologians. Presumably he had people such as the

---

33. Ibid., 197.
34. Ibid., 231-408.

author of *The Shepherd of Hermas*, Evagrius of Pontus, and St Ignatius of Loyola in mind. This kind of discernment requires a good deal of learning and an experiential awareness of spiritual things. Then there was the gift *gratis datae* of discernment mentioned in 1 Cor 12:10 which is a non-permanent gift given to some people whenever God wishes. He defined it as follows: 'The gift of discerning spirits is therefore nothing else but an enlightening of the mind, with which man being endowed, easily and without error decides from what source his own thoughts and those of others, which are subjects of choice, proceed, what is suggested by a good, or evil spirit.'[35] He believed that, whereas the art of discernment would sometimes lead to mistaken conclusions, the charism was infallible. He also said, following St Thomas in *ST* I-II, q. 111, a. 3, that the charism could also take the form of an awareness of the thoughts of another person's heart. Like the charism of prophecy, this ability, which is akin to what contemporary Charismatics refer to as a word of knowledge, can confirm the faith by making known personal secrets known only to God and the individual. He went on to say that Sts Peter of Alcantara and Philip Neri both had been granted this gift. In more recent times, saintly people such as John Vianney, Padre Pio and Anne Catherine Emmerich were among those who had a reputation for exercising this charism. Like the other gifts *gratis datae* it is not necessarily granted to very holy people. In theory it could be given to a wicked person, for the good of another.

b) Speaking in Tongues

It was noted in the chapter on St Thomas's theology of the charisms that he seemed to think that this gift could take the form of *xenoglossi*, i.e. the gift of speaking an unknown language, or *glossolalia*, i.e. a non-conceptual, non-imaginative form of private prayer. It is a curious fact that Bishop Lambertini ignored the latter in favour of the former. On this occasion he took a very didactic, evangelistic approach when he said that 'it [the gift of tongues] is given for the good of others, namely, for the propagation of the faith.'[36] He adverted to the fact that, for good theological reasons, St Thomas thought that *xenoglossi* referred

35. Ibid., 215-16.
36. Ibid., 217.

to the ability of the apostles to speak many languages they did not know, rather than an ability of the hearers to understand the one language spoken by the apostles. He felt that scripture supported such a belief because Paul said in 1 Cor 14:18, 'I thank my God, I speak in tongues [understood as languages] more than any of you.' It can be noted in passing that modern exegetes would not support that understanding of the verse.[37] In spite of Thomas's teaching on the subject, Lambertini thought, like many authorities of his time such as Epagomene Viguier, the Fathers of Salamanca, and Petrus Thyraeus, that it was possible that the gift of tongues may have referred to an ability of the hearers to understand a foreign language. As usual his encyclopedic learning came to his aid and he referred to many instances when this had occurred. For example, when the cause of St Francis Xavier was being examined by the Rota in Rome, the official report said, 'Xavier was illustrious for the gift of tongues, for he spoke with elegance and fluency the languages, which he had never learnt, of different nations, to whom he went for the sake of preaching the gospel, just as if he had been born and bred among them; and it happened not infrequently, that while he was preaching, men of diverse nations heard him speak each in his own language.'[38]

c) Interpretation of Tongues

Given that Lambertini only interpreted the gift of tongues as *xenoglossi*, his understanding of the gift of the interpretation of tongues was necessarily influenced by that fact. He said that the charism could be understood in two ways, firstly, as an ability to translate the foreign words spoken by an evangelist. Because he was talking about a gift *gratis datae*, it necessarily followed that the gift referred to a supernatural rather than a natural ability to do so. Secondly, he said the gift might not refer to the God given

37. For instance, commenting on this verse, Gordon Fee clearly believes that Paul was referring to *glossolalia* when he says in his commentary *The First Epistle to the Corinthians*, 674, 'Along with vv. 14-15 and 2 Cor 12:1-10, this assertion in v. 18 lets us in on aspects of Paul's personal piety for which we otherwise would have been quite unprepared. Apparently his life of personal devotion was regularly given to praying, singing and praising in tongues.'
38. Ibid., 225.

ability to translate, but rather to a graced ability to 'teach the mysteries which lie hid in the words.'[39] At this point Lambertini was in a *cul de sac* of his own making. He seemed to realize the fact when he wrote, 'In the causes of beatification and canonisation it seems to me extremely difficult for an opportunity to present itself of discussing this grace of interpretation of speeches. For although it may happen, and often does happen, that the hidden mysteries of the scriptures have been explained by a servant of God without human study, this will belong, not to the grace of interpretation of speeches, but to infused knowledge, of which we have spoken before.'[40]

CONCLUSION

Prospero Lambertini's treatment of the charisms is beset by a number of problems. Firstly, because he had so little personal experience of the subjects he wrote about, he was more like a man who was writing an article for an encyclopedia or theological dictionary than a creative theologian. He researched what others had written, such as St Thomas, Francisco Suarez, the Fathers of Salamanca etc, and synthesised their thinking. Although his work demonstrates learning and comprehension, his synthesis demonstrates very little originality.

Secondly there is an inherent tension in his approach, as there is in St Thomas. On the one hand, he was at pains to point out that the exercise of the gifts *gratis datae* was not dependant on personal holiness, but on the other, he failed to explain why it was so little in evidence in the lives of flawed people, clerical and lay, during the preceding centuries. Given his role in the Congregation of Rites, it is understandable that he was interested in the criteria to be used in assessing the lives of people who were put forward for possible beatification and canonisation. Although he said on a number of occasions that the exercise of the gifts *gratis datae* was not in itself a sign of sanctity, nevertheless, if it could be established that the candidate had led a life of heroic virtue, then it would be considered as a divine endorsement of that virtue.

---

39. Ibid., 228.
40. Ibid., 231.

Thirdly, although Lambertini was clearly a disciple of St Thomas, he did not adopt his classification of the charisms and the sound theological reasons he had for doing so. Instead, he studied the charisms in a sequential way. It is true that he did so in groups of gifts, but he said precious little about the criteria he used in making those groupings. So, while St Thomas put forward a powerful evangelistic interpretation of the gifts *gratis datae*, Lambertini did not do so. However, as has been noted above, he often commented in passing, on the evangelising dimension of the charisms in 1 Cor 12:8-10. For example, he put an exaggerated and questionable emphasis on the role of *xenoglossi* in proclaiming the good news. But it appears to me that he failed to do so within a coherent and explicit theological framework.

Fourthly, while the writings of St Thomas demonstrated a great reliance on scripture and the kinds of scriptural exegesis current at his time, Lambertini did not do so. Of course he did refer to scripture texts, but the reader does not get the impression that he was *au fait* with their significance in the same way as St Thomas. As was noted earlier, he seemed to adopt the notion of the 'utterance of faith' in an uncritical way. Had he been familiar with the Greek text, he may not have interpreted the charism of faith (1 Cor 12:9) in such a didactic way. It was noted in chapter two that a number of modern exegetes have warned Charismatics that, because they rely so heavily on their own experience as a theological hermeneutic, they may interpret what Paul says about the gifts in an unjustifiable way. Reading Lambertini, it is obvious that the converse is also true. If personal experience is absent, the interpretation of reports of charismatic activity in the lives of others, whether in scripture, the Fathers of the Church, or the lives of saints, can be quite mistaken. For instance, although it is referred to in scripture (1 Cor 14:14), it is fairly obvious that Lambertini did not understand the charism of speaking in tongues as a private prayer gift. It is not surprising that he did not understand the gift of the interpretation of tongues either.

In spite of these caveats, Prospero Lambertini's account of the charisms is not only significant, especially in view of the fact that later on he became the Pope, it is also very helpful. It represents a good summary of many of the best insights of the

Catholic tradition to do with the more unusual gifts of the Spirit. Even if he did not adopt St Thomas's didactic and evangelistic interpretation in its entirety, he did make many useful comments in passing about the interdependence of gifts of revelation, proclamation and demonstration in effective evangelisation.

CHAPTER FIVE

The decline and re-emergence
of the Gifts of the Spirit

The role of the charisms in evangelisation is sometimes mentioned by the post-apostolic fathers of the church (50-150 AD
aprox.) such as Justin, Irenaeus, Tertullian, Origen and Cyprian.
For instance, St Irenaeus wrote in the second century: 'For some
do certainly and truly drive out devils, so that those who have
thus been cleansed from evil spirits frequently join themselves
to the church. Others have foreknowledge of things to come:
they see visions, and utter prophecies. Others still, heal the sick
by laying their hands upon them, and they are made whole. Yes,
moreover, as I have said, the dead even have been raised up,
and remained among us for many years. And what more shall I
say? It is not possible to name the number of the gifts which the
church throughout the whole world, has received from God, in
the name of Jesus Christ.'[1] In the 4th century St Hilary of Poitiers
wrote in a commentary on Ps 64: 'We who are reborn through
the sacrament of baptism have the greatest joy, as we perceive
within us the first stirrings of the Holy Spirit, as we begin to understand mysteries; we gain full knowledge of prophecy, speech
full of wisdom, security in our hope, and gifts of healing and
dominion over devils who are made subject to us.'[2]

Book eight of the *Apostolic Constitutions*, which was written
in the 4th century, talks about the gifts of the Spirit and how
these demonstrations of God's power support the proclamation
of the gospel to unbelievers: 'Let not, therefore,' its author says,
'any one that works signs and wonders judge any one of the
faithful who is not granted the same: for the gifts of God which
are bestowed by him through Christ are various; and one man
receives one gift, and another a different gift. For perhaps one

1. *Against Heresies* 2:32; 4.
2. Tract on Psalm 64:15; CSEL.

91

has the word of wisdom, and another the word of knowledge; another, discerning of spirits; another, foreknowledge of things to come; another, the word of teaching; another, long-suffering; another, continence according to the law ... These gifts were first bestowed on us the apostles when we were about to preach the gospel to every creature, and afterwards were of necessity afforded to those who had by our means believed; not for the advantage of those who perform them, *but for the conviction of the unbelievers, that those whom the word did not persuade, the power of signs might put to shame* [my italics]: for signs are not for us who believe, but for the unbelievers, both for the Jews and Gentiles ... Wherefore let none of you exalt himself against his brother, though he be a prophet, or though he be a worker of miracles: for if it happens that there be no longer an unbeliever, all the power of signs will thenceforwards be superfluous.'[3] Two points can be made about that final observation. It seems to imply a cessationist theory whereby the gifts would be withdrawn in a Christian society. However, it also implies that in a secular society like ours, where there are many unbelievers, we have good reason to expect that the gifts of the Spirit will be restored as a support to our evangelisation.

In a book entitled, *Christianizing the Roman Empire*, Ramsay Mac Mullen, a professor of history and classics at Yale University has written: 'When careful assessment is made of passages in the ancient written evidence that clearly indicate [a] motive ... leading a person to conversion, they show (so far as I can discover): first, the operation of a desire for blessings ... second, and much more attested, a fear of physical pain ... third, and most frequent, credence in miracles'[4] Apparently, what most impressed the people who were converted, especially the poor and uneducated of the time, were healings and especially exorcisms.

DECLINE OF THE GIFTS OF THE SPIRIT

There is good reason to believe that the Montanist movement in the second century may have contributed to the decline of

3. Book 8, part I, 'Diversity of spiritual gifts.' It is thought that this part of Book 8 may have been written by St Hippolytus at an earlier time.
4. (New Haven: Yale University Press, 1984), 108

charismatic activity in the church. Montanus and his two colleagues, Priscilla and Maximilla, were inspired by the line, 'I will
send you the advocate, the spirit of truth' (Jn 15:26). They maintained that they were receiving visions and prophetic revelations directly from the Spirit which even superceded those of
the New Testament in significance. Tertullian was their best
known supporter. The church eventually condemned Montanism
and as a result, the exercise of the gifts of the Spirit became suspect. There was a tendency instead to stress the role of the scriptures and the teaching authority of the bishops as the successors
of the apostles.

Later in the 4th century, it is clear in the writings of Sts John
Chrysostom and Augustine of Hippo that the gifts of the Spirit
were no longer in evidence. For example, Chrysostom said with
great candor: 'This whole passage 1 Cor 12:8-12 is very obscure;
but *the obscurity is produced by our ignorance of the facts referred to,*
[my italics] and by their cessation, being such as then used to
occur, but now no longer take place.'[5] Both men seemed to accept the cessationist point of view which maintained that the
gifts of the Spirit were granted by God in order to get the church
established. But once the different forms of clerical ministry
were operating, the sacraments were being administered, and
dioceses established, the gifts were no longer needed. As a result, they were withdrawn by God. It should be noted, however,
that Augustine changed his mind on this specific point in his
Retractions, which he wrote toward the end of his life.[6] He quoted
words he had written in *The True Religion,* 'These miracles are
not allowed to continue into our time, lest the soul should always require things that can be seen, and by becoming accus-
tomed to them mankind should grow cold towards the very
thing whose novelty had made men glow with fire.' Having
heard reliable accounts of healings in his diocese of Hippo,
Augustine stated in his *Retractions* (426-28), 'What I said should
not be taken as understanding that no miracles are believed to
happen today in the name of Christ.'

---

5. Homily, XXIX on 1 Corinthians, http://www.newadvent.org/fathers
/220129.htm (accessed on May 2nd 2008)
6. On Augustine's attitudes see, Morton Kelsey, *Healing & Christianity*
(London: SCM, 1973), 185.

In the last few hundred years other cultural influences have militated against the exercise of the gifts of the Spirit. The rise of science, and the Newtonian notion of a closed universe also had a detrimental effect. As David Hume and others tried to show, miracles are an *a priori* impossibility. In Sec. 10, par. 90 of his *Enquiry Concerning Human Understanding* (1748), Hume wrote: 'The many instances of forged miracles, and prophecies, and supernatural events, which, in all ages, have either been detected by contrary evidence, or which detect themselves by their absurdity, prove sufficiently the strong propensity of mankind to the extraordinary and marvellous, and ought reasonably to begat a suspicion against all relations of this kind.'

Christian scholars have been influenced by the scientific worldview. For instance, Rudolf Bultmann, one of the most influential students of the Bible of the 20th century, espoused a naturalistic perspective. As a result he, like some other Christian thinkers, maintained that New Testament stories recounting signs and wonders should be demythologised. In a series of lectures delivered at US seminaries in 1951, he reinforced the presupposition that the New Testament worldview is mythical: 'The whole conception of the world which is presupposed in the preaching of Jesus as in the New Testament generally is mythological; i.e. the conception of the world as being structured in three stories, heaven, earth, and hell; the conception of the intervention of supernatural powers in the course of events; and the conception of miracles, especially the conception of the intervention of supernatural powers in the inner life of the soul, the conception that men can be tempted and corrupted by the devil and possessed by evil spirits.'[7] This tendency is quite evident in some contemporary writing about the existence of the devil and the legitimacy of exorcism. For example, in his commentary on Ephesians (Eph 6:10-17), Lionel Swain, a Catholic scripture scholar says: 'Warfare – even spiritual warfare – is not a metaphor that is very congenial to our modern mentality, especially when we realise that belligerent spiritual forces outside man are part of an outmoded cosmology.'[8]

---

7. *Jesus Christ and Mythology* (New Jersey: Prentice Hall: 1997), 15.
8. (Dublin: Veritas, 1980), 105.

THE OCCASIONAL RE-APPEARANCE OF THE GIFTS OF THE SPIRIT

Despite the decline in charismatic activity from the fourth century onwards, the gifts of the Spirit continued to be exercised by some exceptionally gifted saints and by a few less than saintly people.

There were many of them, I'm sure, but one case I discovered by accident really interested me. Alvar Nunez Cabeza De Vaca and some Spanish explorers were shipwrecked in North America between 1528-1536. It is fascinating to read about their interaction with the Indians and especially De Vaca's healing ministry. Surely it has significance for a number of reasons. Although there are clear indications that he was a good man and a devout Christian he was not a saint. Nevertheless, he exercised the charism of healing at a time when it was quite exceptional.

Secondly, there seemed to be a providential significance in the fact that the very first Christians in America were healers.

Thirdly, Cabeza had told the Indians that, as a Christian, he believed in the true God. They were pragmatic in their response. They said that if the Christian God was all powerful, as the Spaniards maintained, then they should pray to their God for healing. When the credibility of their beliefs was challenged in this way, Cabeza felt that he couldn't let Christianity down. So relying on God's power he prayed for healing, and it occurred time and time again.

For instance, in one place he makes this extraordinary claim: 'As we drew near the huts of the afflicted, I saw that the man we hoped to save was dead: many mourners were weeping around him, and his house was already down [to be burned with the deceased's possessions] – sure signs that the inhabitant was no more. I found his eyes rolled up, his pulse gone, and every appearance of death ... Taking off the mat that covered him, I supplicated our Lord in his behalf and in behalf of the rest who ailed, as fervently as I could ... that evening, they brought the tidings that the "dead" man I had treated had got up whole and walked; he had eaten and spoken with these Sosulas, who further reported that all I had ministered to had recovered and were glad.

Throughout the land the effect was a profound wonder and fear. People talked of nothing else, and wherever the fame of it reached, people set out to find us so we should cure them and bless their children.'[9]

At this point, however, we will focus on examples of the gifts of the Spirit in the remarkable lives of four canonised saints, Anthony of the Desert, Francis of Assisi, Vincent Ferrer and Francis of Paola. They are necessarily brief and impressionistic.

a) St Anthony of the desert

St Athanasius (293-273), wrote a life of St Anthony (251-356)[10] who lived at a time that the church had to contend with paganism, the threat of the Arian heresy, and a watering down of the ideals that had informed the first Christians. He depicted Anthony as a remarkable man of God who exercised many of the gifts of the Spirit. He had gifts of revelation, proclamation and demonstration.

We are informed that if there was something he did not know, 'the Lord would reveal it to him as he prayed; and he was, as it says in scripture, taught by God.'[11] Later on Athanasius adds, 'Anthony was able to perceive each person's misfortune for he had been granted the gift of discerning spirits on account of his virtuous life.'[12] He received prophetic foreknowledge from God. For instance, Athanasius recounted a story about a young girl from Busiris who suffered from an unknown and pitiable disease. Besides dripping pus from her ears, she was paralysed and cross-eyed. When monks tried to tell him about the girl's condition, Anthony was able to describe it in detail. Then he said to the monks: 'Go and you will find the girl healed … This girl, for whom you ask my help, has been released as a result of her own prayers; when I prayed to the Lord, I was granted foreknowledge of her cure.'

Not long after this incident, two monks were travelling to see Anthony. They ran out of water. One of them died of thirst,

---

9. *The Journey and Ordeal of Cabeza de Vaca: His Account of the Disastrous First European Exploration of the American Southwest*, trs and ed, Cyclone Covey (New York: Dover, 2003), 88-89. De Vaca got back to Europe and wrote the account of his adventures to the King of Spain.
10. *Early Christian Lives*, trs & ed, Carolinne White (London: Penguin Books, 1988), 3-70.
11. Ibid., 50.
12. Idid., 64.

while the other was nearing death. Anthony called two monks and told them to bring water to a person on the road leading to Egypt. He said to them: 'One of the brothers who is on his way here has just passed away to the Lord; the other will do so, too, unless you help him. This was revealed to me just now as I was praying.' On yet another occasion, Anthony had a visionary experience where he saw a soul moving heavenward accompanied by the angels. Immediately a voice said to him that this was the soul of a monk called Ammon who lived in Nitria, some thirteen days away. This knowledge filled him with joy. When he was asked why he was so cheerful he told them that Ammon, a miracle worker, had just died. Later on Anthony, now a very old man, predicted his own death.

Anthony was a hermit who did not expect that he would have occasion to preach. But when people began to know about the holiness of this remarkable warrior of God, who had overcome all the wiles of the devil, they flocked to hear him. Athanasius tells that, 'His speech seasoned with salt, brought comfort to those who grieved, instructed the ignorant, reconciled those who were angry and persuaded everyone that nothing should be valued higher than the love of Christ. He would set before their eyes the great number of future rewards as well as the mercy of God, and he made known the benefits granted because God did not spare his own Son but had given him for the salvation of us all. His words had the immediate effect of persuading many of those who heard him to reject human things: this began the beginning of the desert's colonisation.'[13] St Athanasius also tells us that, in spite of his lack of formal learning, Anthony was a great apologist for the Catholic faith. He was able to argue effectively against the Arian heresy and to answer the questions of pagan philosophers who came to dialogue with him. We are told that 'the philosophers went away, amazed at his mental acuteness and at his ability.'[14]

It is quite evident that St Anthony not only proclaimed the gospel, he demonstrated its truth by means of deeds of power. Athanasius exclaimed at one point, 'How many people were freed from the devil's grip and from many different illnesses at

13. Idid., 19.
14. Ibid., 54.

that time.'[15] On one occasion Anthony was asked to pray for some monks who were about to set sail in a boat. When he got on board he said he was aware of a foul smell. The men in the boat said it was the odour of rotting fish. Anthony maintained it was something else. 'While he was still speaking, a young man in the grip of a demon, who had slipped ahead beside the hull and hidden himself in the boat, suddenly cried out. Anthony immediately cured him in the name of our Lord Jesus Christ and all the people realised that it was the devil who had given off the foul smell.'[16] On another occasion when journeying trough the hot and arid desert he, his companions and their camel were dying of thirst. We are told that Anthony 'knelt down, and stretched out his hands in supplication to the Lord. Without delay, as soon as the tears fell from his eyes, there burst forth a bubbling spring in the exact spot where he was praying and when they had quenched their thirst and cooled their burning limbs, they filled their water-skins and then found the camel and let it drink.'[17] Apparently Anthony feared that all the miracles granted to him might either make him proud or induce others to have a higher estimation of him than was warranted. But as for the people, 'they were shocked and terrified by Anthony to whom God was granting, in addition to such wisdom, the ability to perform miracles.'[18] As a result of his evangelisation, Anthony became the father of the monastic movement, an effective enemy of Arianism and someone who edified believers.

b) St Francis of Assisi

Centuries later, St Bonaventure (1221-1274) wrote a remarkable life of St Francis of Assisi (1181-1226) who lived at a time when Italy was war torn. Indeed, in 1201, Francis joined a military expedition against Perugia. He was taken as a prisoner at Collestrada, and spent a year as a captive.[19] That event probably kick-started his conversion experience. Bonaventure's biography set out to show that the *povarello* was a Christ-like figure,

---

15. Idid., 53
16. Ibid., 48.
17. Ibid., 42.
18. Ibid., 59.
19. *The Life of St Francis of Assisi* (Rockford, Ill.: Tan Books, 1988).

who not only bore Christ's wounds in his body, he also preached in an anointed way and exercised the gifts of the Spirit like his Master.

It is clear, that although he had very little formal education in either scripture or theology, Francis, like Anthony before him, was blessed by revelation from God that transcended human knowledge. Bonaventure says that: 'he foresaw the ruin of many who appeared likely to persevere; and on the contrary, predicted with assured certainty the conversion of many sinners to Christ.' He gives many examples. For instance, two friars came to visit him. While on the way, the elder one gave scandal to the younger. When they arrived, Francis asked them how the journey had gone. The younger friar said, 'Very well,' but Francis responded: 'Take heed, brother, lest you tell a lie under the semblance of humility, for I know what I know, but wait a while and you shall see.' The young friar was astonished to see that the Spirit had revealed to Francis what had really happened. Apparently, a few days later, the elder man, who had given scandal, departed 'in contempt of religion'. Bonaventure concludes, 'In the ruin of this one man two things were made manifest – the divine justice, and the prophetic gift of St Francis.'

For a time Francis was not sure whether he should devote himself to preaching. 'Which, my brethren,' he said (to his fellow friars), 'do you advise me to do – to give myself wholly to prayer, or to go about preaching the gospel? For I, being a poor sinful man, and unskilled in preaching, have received the gift of prayer, rather than of speech.'[20] St Bonaventure tells us that it was revealed to his companions from on high that it was 'the good pleasure of God that the servant of Christ should go forth and preach.'[21] Having been called by God to proclaim the good news, Francis's words were blessed. We are told that 'wherever he went there was ever present that Spirit of the Lord, who had sent him forth; and the power and wisdom of Christ were with him, making him to abound in words of true and wholesome doctrine.'[22]

20. Idid., 112.
21. Ibid., 113.
22. Ibid., 116.

St Bonaventure says that wherever Francis spoke, 'the Lord working with him confirmed his word with signs.'[23] The healings, miracles and exorcisms were quite amazing. His biographer supplies us with numerous examples in chapter twelve. They ranged from curing people with distorted limbs, restoring sight, and ending epileptic fits. He also drove out evil spirits from people and whole towns. We are told that 'in the city of Castello a furious and malignant spirit, who had entered into a woman, having received a command from the holy man, departed in great wrath, leaving the woman whom he had possessed free in both body and mind.'[24] There is also an interesting account about his visit to war-torn Arezzo. 'He saw a multitude of demons rejoicing over the city, and instigating the angry citizens to destroy each other.' He said to brother Sylvester, 'Go to the gates of the city, and there, in the name of Almighty God, command the demons by virtue of holy obedience, that without delay they depart from that place.' As soon as brother Sylvester carried out Francis's instructions, 'the tumult of the city was appeased.'[25] Bonaventure concludes, 'The herald of Christ being thus glorified by these and many other miracles, men listened to the things which he said in his preaching, as if an angel of the Lord were speaking to them.'[26] As a result of his evangelisation, Francis inaugurated the eponymous movement that bears his name, reconciliation and a general renewal of Christian belief and mores.

c) Vincent Ferrer

Born in Spain, Vincent Ferrer (1350-1419) was the son of an Anglo-Scottish father and a Spanish mother. He lived at a time when the church in Europe was in a bad way as a result of the great schism (1378-1417) during which no less than three men claimed to be the Pope. This scandalous situation weakened ecclesiastical authority, divided the faithful and weakened faith. In his native country Moslems were very influential. Clearly there was a need for a new evangelisation. A third of the European

---

23. Ibid., 117.
24. Ibid., 119.
25. Ibid., 61.
26. Ibid., 120.

population died in the black death, others died on the crusades or in the 100 years war.

As one biographer indicates, the gifts Vincent, a Dominican priest, exercised were no less impressive than those that were evident in the lives of Anthony and Francis.[27] He was clearly endowed with gifts of revelation. He himself said: 'Be thoroughly persuaded, that true revelations, and the extraordinary means by which God's secrets are known, are not the result of the desire, nor of any diligence or effort on the part of the soul itself; but that they are solely the effects of the pure goodness of God communicating itself to a soul filled with humility, who respectfully seeks for him and sighs after him with all its strength.' Andrew Pradel, one of his biographers, says that 'his gift of reading hearts was truly miraculous.' For example, when he was preaching, people in the crowd would sometimes throw folded pieces of paper on to the platform. They contained questions they wanted the saintly Dominican to answer. The following day he would respond to the questions in detail without having ever looked at the pieces of paper. There is a story which demonstrated Vincent's remarkable spiritual gifts. On one occasion he was travelling through the Basque region. In one place he met a man who was being led out to execution. At the same time a funeral procession was passing. Knowing by inspiration that the condemned man was innocent, Vincent called on the corpse to testify to the fact. The dead man sat up, pronounced the other innocent, and fell back again. At one point in his life Vincent Ferrer wrote a short *Treatise on the Spiritual Life*. Chapter thirteen contains very sage advice on how to distinguish a true from a false revelation from God.[28]

Vincent had a remarkable gift for proclaiming the good news. At the age of 51 Pope Benedict XIII appointed him as ambassador extraordinary of Christ. He had authority to preach everywhere; no diocese, city, or church could be closed to him. For the next 18 years he travelled the length and breadth of Europe four times. He visited Ireland, England and Scotland. He

---

27. *Angel of the Judgment: A Life of Vincent Ferrer* (Notre Dame, In: Ave Maria Press, 1954)
28. http://www.theotokos.org.uk/pages/appdisce/vferrer.html Accessed Sept 25th 2008.

usually preached the gospel once or twice a day. Apparently his scripture based sermons could last anything up to three hours! [29] In a sermon he preached on the feast of Sts Peter and Paul, he said: 'Preaching is like a net, because just as with a net all is collected and it is drawn by one cord, so evangelical preaching uses several cords, namely, authorities, reasons, and parables, and all are collected. If preaching is well organised, and they draw one cord, namely the theme, which is the basis of a sermon, God sends those kind of preachers.'[30] Prospero Lambertini, later Pope Benedict XIV, said in his four volume *De Servorum Dei Beatificatione, et Beatorum Canonizatione* that St Antoninus of Florence had recounted how the gift of *xenoglossi* was granted to St Vincent Ferrer: 'This was astonishing, and an apostolic grace, that preaching in Catalonia in the common language of the country, he was understood by other nations who knew it not.'[31] When one reads his life story it becomes clear that Vincent was the Billy Graham of his day. Up to three or four thousand people, including many women, followed him from place to place, and he drew big crowds wherever he went.

Besides being an inspired and inspiring preacher, Ferrer performed many deeds of power. As one contemporary said: 'Every step was a miracle, every word a victory for heaven.' Pradel points out that whenever he finished preaching he would heal the sick and reconcile those who were at enmity with each other. For example at a place called Ferusasco, a woman brought him her child who was suffering from epilepsy. With the touch of his hand the condition was cured. On another occasion he went to Lyon and preached at Saint-Synphorien d'Auzon. We are told that the number of sick people who came to him every day was so great that it was impossible to count them. At certain times he visited the sick who were housebound. He laid hands upon them and recited prayers, and cured them. In every town and village where Ferrer ministered conversions were large and usually lasting. Feuds were brought to an end, people were rec-

29. For examples of his sermons see http://www.svfparish.org/svfsermons/index.htm (accessed Sept. 25th 2008).
30. http://www.svfparish.org/svfsermons/C246_On%20St.%20Peter.htm (accessed Sept 25th 2008).
31. Prospero Lambertini, *Heroic Virtue*, 224.

onciled with one another, prostitutes were cleared from the streets, priests returned to pastoral care of parishioners, and people devoted themselves to God in a conscientious way. St Vincent Ferrer is the patron saint of builders because of his fame for 'building up' and strengthening the church

d) Francis of Paola

Francis of Paola (1416-1507) was a remarkable child from the day of his birth until the day of his death, ninety-one years later. He came into the world at a time when the Western schism was still dividing the church. There were three men claiming to be Pope, Gregory XII, Benedict XIII, and John XXIII. Furthermore, Europe was subject to regular attacks by the Turks. It would seem that Francis was truly holy from an early age. He had been healed of an eye complaint when his parents prayed fervently to St Francis Assisi. Later he received his education from the local Franciscans. From his teenage years onwards he was noted for the intensity of his prayer and ascetical practices. Like other saintly people he suffered and overcame great temptations from the devil. He said on one occasion: 'The devil, believe me, has a consuming hatred against the servants of Christ. The malignant one, seeing that he cannot steal their souls, vents his most terrible wrath on them, forcing them to cope with every kind of suffering.'[32] Francis lived as a hermit for a number of years. During that time companions joined him and later they formed the Hermits of St Francis of Assisi, who were given the name of the Minim Friars. After the approval of the order, Francis founded several new monasteries in Calabria and Sicily. He also established convents of nuns, and a third order for people living in the world, after the example of St Francis of Assisi. Apparently he was a superb organiser, administrator and leader.

It is obvious when reading about Francis that he was blessed with remarkable prophetic gifts. Like Anthony, Francis, and Vincent before him, he had a God-given ability to foretell future events and to read hearts. For instance, he foretold the capture of Otranto by the Ottoman Turks in 1480, and its subsequent recov-

---

32. Gino J. Simi and Mario M. Segreti, *St Francis of Paola: God's Miracle Worker Supreme* (Rockford, Ill.: Tan Books, 1977), 23.

ery by the King of Naples. On another occasion there was a con-
flict known as the Tuscan war. When he was asked what was
likely to happen Francis replied, 'Have no fears; before you
know it, the belligerents will come to an understanding.' Soon
afterwards this prophecy was fulfilled when Lorenzo de Medici
and the King of Naples came to terms. He was also known to
have given prophetic advice to farmers in Paola. For instance, he
told one of his friends to buy lots of grain when it was very
cheap. The next year the harvest failed due to a drought, but his
friend had so much stored up that he could supply the needs of
the local people.

Although he did not feel called to dedicate himself to evangelisation as St Francis of Assisi did, he was active in the
apostolate. He was a friend of the poor by speaking up for them
and pleading their cause with the secular authorities of the day.
When occasion required it, he would courageously challenge
their attitudes and unjust actions without fear. When news of
Francis's sanctity spread he was consulted by a number of Popes
and kings. As a result he had an opportunity of evangelising,
usually by encouraging them to repent in one way or another
and to walk in the ways of the Lord. In one of his letters he
wrote: 'You are well aware that our sins arouse God's anger.
You must change your life, therefore, so that God in his mercy
will pardon you. What we conceal from men is known to God.
Be converted, then, with a sincere heart. Live your life that you
may receive the blessing of the Lord. Then the peace of God our
Father will be with you always.' When he met the King of
Naples he was not afraid to call him to repentance: 'Sire, your
people are oppressed and made miserable by your government,
which is an affront to God and mankind. Throughout your kingdom there is great suffering that is obvious and general.'[33] The
admonition had its desired effect and King Ferrante promised to
change. When the French King, Louis XI, suffered a debilitating
stroke which robbed him of his speech and left him partly paralysed, understandably he was very frightened. He had heard of
Francis and asked him to come and minister to him. The saint,
who was sixty-five at the time, did not think it was God's will

---

33. Ibid., 112.

for him to go, so he declined the request. He changed his mind, however, when the Pope Sixtus IV intervened and asked him to go. Francis told Louis that what God wanted was for the king to become a firm believer and a true Christian. It was not a message the king wanted to hear. He used every kind of persuasion to induce the saint to cure him. Eventually the cynical sovereign understood what the saint was trying to get across, that he had to concern himself with his soul rather than his body. Finally the king died on Saturday 30 Aug 1483. His biographer wrote: 'I have never seen any man die so peacefully.' Francis also helped to broker peace between France and Brittany, by advising a marriage between the ruling families, and between France and Spain, by persuading Louis XI to return some disputed land.

It would not be an exaggeration to say that Francis of Paola was probably the greatest miracle worker the church has ever known. His amazing deeds are too many to recount. Here are just two of many, many possible examples. On one occasion a Papal Legate called Monsignor Adorno was sent to visit Francis. The saint had requested the Pontiff to grant his order permission to follow the Lenten fast throughout the year, i.e. not eating such things as meat, eggs and dairy produce. The legate said: 'I must point out that this extreme form of self-mortification is inconsistent with the demands of human nature, and is therefore condemned by the wisest men of our age.'[34] Francis listened calmly to what the visitor from Rome had to say. Then he arose, walked over to a brazier, and with both hands scooped up the burning embers. With the coals glowing brightly, he held them out to the astonished Monsignor. The saint commented, 'Yes it is true Monsignor, I am not only an unlearned peasant, and if I were not, I would not be able to do this.'[35] Mgr Adorno got the message. When he returned to Rome, he told the Pope that the stories that he had heard about Francis's miraculous powers had not been exaggerated. In 1483, when Francis arrived in France, he visited a city called Bormes which was in the grip of the plague. Francis asked to be brought to the nearest hospital. He blessed the afflicted and all of them were cured! Soon after-

34. Ibid., 60
35. Ibid., 61

wards the pestilence ceased to infect any of the inhabitants. On his way to the cathedral in another town called Frejus he met a woman and asked her why there were so few people to be seen. She explained that the plague was ravaging the population. Up to half of them had already died. He responded by saying that he was there to help. When the people heard that the Calabrian saint was at the governor's palace, they gathered there. Francis made the sign of the cross over the afflicted and they all recovered. The city was soon freed of the disease.

Shortly after Francis of Paola's death, there were insistent requests from France and Italy for his canonisation. Evidence was gathered between 1516 and 1518 when 120 witnesses were interviewed. They spoke about the many healings and miracles Francis had performed including raising dead people and animals to life, and walking on water.[36] He was canonised a mere twelve years after his death, in 1519.

THE RE-EMERGENCE OF THE GIFTS OF THE SPIRIT

During the twentieth century a dramatic restoration of the gifts of the Spirit took place, in three interrelated stages of revival: firstly, the Pentecostal Movement, secondly the Charismatic Movements and finally the Signs and Wonders Movement. As you may know, the first stage of renewal occurred in the form of the Pentecostal revival which took place in Azuza Street in 1906 when a group of poorer people from diverse backgrounds and races were baptised in the Holy Spirit and exercised the gifts of the Spirit which are mentioned in 1 Cor 12:8-10. When they were rejected by the mainline churches, they formed their own churches and spread out across the world to bring the Pentecostal message to others.

Smith Wigglesworth, an Englishman, was one of the first Pentecostals in Britain. He was baptised in the Holy Spirit in 1907. In 1937 he visited South Africa as a guest of the Apostolic Faith Mission in Johannesburg. David Du Plessis was its general secretary at the time. Later, Du Plessis explained how one morning, Wigglesworth walked, unannounced, into his office. He

---

36. Franz Liszt wrote a piano piece entitled, 'St Francis of Paola Walking on the Waves.' It can be heard on http://www.youtube.com/watch?v=vl-1rueI1GA

pushed him against the wall and declared: 'You have been in Jerusalem long enough ... I will send you to the uttermost parts of the earth ... You will bring the message of Pentecost to all churches ... You will travel more than most evangelists do ... God is going to revive the churches in the last days and through them turn the world upside down ... even the Pentecostal movement will become a mere joke compared with the revival which God will bring through the churches.' After a pause Wigglesworth continued: 'Then the Lord said to me that I am warning you that he is going to use you in this movement ... All he requires of you is that you be humble and faithful. You will live to see this word fulfilled.' Then he concluded by saying that this prophecy about the second phase of blessing would not be fulfilled until after his death. In the event, Wigglesworth died in 1947.

Over the next few years Du Plessis became increasingly influential in Protestant and later in Catholic circles. The Protestant Charismatic Movement began when influential people like Episcopal priest, Dennis Bennett, and Lutheran pastor, Larry Christenson were baptised in the Spirit and began to exercise the gifts of the Spirit in the early 60s. In his book *Simple and Profound*, Du Plessis described how he first made contact with Catholics. At a gathering in St Andrews in Scotland, in 1951, he met Professor Bernard Lemming, a Jesuit priest from Oxford. He asked for prayer for baptism in the Holy Spirit. This marked the start of Du Plessis's ministry to Catholics. When the Second Vatican Council started, Du Plessis was invited to attend.

The growth of the modern Catholic Charismatic Movement was anticipated, in a prophetic way, when the Second Vatican Council discussed the subject of lay ministry and the charisms of the Holy Spirit. There were two schools of thought. The traditionalists, led by Cardinal Rufini, adopted the cessationist point of view when they argued that the charisms were granted to the early church in order to get it firmly established. When Christianity took root in the Greco-Roman world, the charisms mentioned in 1 Cor 12:8-10 were no longer needed, and died out rather quickly. Ever since, these particular charisms have been extremely rare and only granted to exceptionally holy people in order to confirm their sanctity and to manifest the divine presence and power.[37] The progressives, led by Cardinal Suenens, argued in an influential speech that there was a spectrum of charisms ranging from the commonplace to the more remarkable.[38] Many of these, especially the more ordinary gifts were already widely dispersed among the faithful for the edification of the church.[39] It should be noted that this approach had been anticipated by Pius XII, in par. 17 of his encyclical *Mysticii Corporis*.[40]

In the event, the second point of view which was supported by scripture scholars attending the Council, prevailed. The main teaching of the bishops was expressed in part two of paragraph twelve of the *Dogmatic Constitution on the Church* (hereafter *LG*). It was reiterated in paragraph three of the *Constitution on the Laity* (hereafter *AA*). The Council's teaching can be summarised in the following eleven points;

1 Grace comes to us primarily through sacraments and clerical ministry (*LG* 12).

2 Grace also comes through the charisms mentioned in 1 Cor 12:8-10 (*LG* 12).

3 The Holy Spirit distributes simple and exceptional gifts, among lay people (*LG* 12; *AA* 3).

4 These gifts are given to build up the church in holiness and to develop people (*LG* 12; *AA* 3).

5 The charisms are a wonderful means of apostolic vitality (*LG* 12).

6 These gifts are to be received with gratitude and consolation (*LG* 12).

7 In virtue of baptism, lay people have a fundamental right to exercise their charisms (*AA* 3).

---

37. See St Thomas in *ST*, II-II, q 178, A2.

38. In her useful book *The Catholic Spiritual Gifts Inventory*, (Colorado Springs: The Siena Institute Press, 1998), Sherry Weddell makes no real distinction between ordinary and extraordinary gifts. My book concentrates on the more extraordinary gifts in 1 Cor 12:8-10 which in Latin are referred to as *gratis datae*.

39. Cardinal Leon Suenens, 'The Charismatic Dimension of the Church', *Council Speeches of Vatican II*, ed. Hans Küng, Yves Congar OP, Daniel O' Hanlon SJ (New Jersey: Deus Books, 1964), 29-34; Albert Vanhoye SJ, 'The Biblical Question of 'Charisms' After Vatican Two,' *Vatican II: Assessment and Perspectives: Twenty-Five Years After* (1962-1987), vol 1. ed. R. Latourelle (New York: Paulist Press, 1988), 442-444.

40. *AAS* 35 (1943), 20.

8   Lay people have a duty to use their charisms for the good of the church and the world (*AA* 3).
9   Bishops and clergy should test the charisms to see that they are genuine and used for the common good (*LG* 12; *AA* 3).
10 The clergy should be careful not to quench the Spirit by an arbitrary use of authority (*LG* 12; *AA* 3).
11 Extraordinary gifts are not to be rashly sought after (*LG* 12).

In the years immediately after the Council, Paul VI often commented on the meaning and implications of these conciliar teachings.[41] In more recent years, Pope John Paul II reiterated the Conciliar teaching in par. 24 of the post-synodal apostolic exhortation, *The Vocation and Mission of the Laity* and in pars. 799-801 and 2003 of the *CCC*. Pope Paul VI said in 1973, 'The breath-giving influence of the Spirit has come to awaken latent forces within the church, to stir up forgotten charisms.'[42] Pope John Paul II clearly rejected the cessationist theory when he said: 'At the beginning of the Christian era extraordinary things were accomplished under the influence of charisms ... This has always been the case in the church and is so in our own day as well.'[43] Pope Benedict has also spoken in a positive manner about the revival of charismatic activity. When he was still Cardinal Prefect of the Congregation for the Doctrine of the Faith, he issued an *Instruction on Prayers for Healing*, which gave qualified approval, in par. 5, of the exercise of the charism of healing by lay people. On another occasion he said: 'In the heart of a world adversely affected by rationalistic skepticism, a new experience of the Holy Spirit has come about, amounting to a worldwide renewal movement. What the New Testament describes with reference to the charisms as visible signs of the coming of the Spirit is no longer merely ancient, past history: this history is becoming a burning reality today.'[44]

41. *Pope Paul VI and the Spirit*, ed. Edward J. O' Connor (Notre Dame, Indiana: Ave Maria Press, 1978).
42. Ibid., 201.
43. *L'Osservatore Romano*, (March 16, 1994).
44. Robert Moynihan, *Let God's Light Shine Forth: The Spiritual Vision of Benedict XVI* (London: Hutchinson, 2005), 101-102.

CONCLUSION

The Catholic Charismatic Renewal came into existence in 1967. From that time onwards the Spirit and the charisms have been poured out in abundance on Catholics, firstly in the US, and later around the world. A unique gathering of ecclesial communities, including charismatic ones, took place in Rome at Pentecost, 30 May 1998. It is estimated that about 200,000 people were present. Speaking on that occasion, Pope John Paul II said: 'Today, I would like to cry out to all of you gathered here in St Peter's Square and to all Christians: Open yourselves docilely to the gifts of the Spirit! Accept gracefully and obediently the charisms which the Spirit never ceases to bestow on us! Do not forget that every charism is given for the common good, that is, for the benefit of the whole church.' At the end of his address, the Pope said: 'Today, from this square, Christ says to each of you: "Go into all the world and preach the gospel to the whole creation" (Mk 16:15). He is counting on every one of you, and so is the church. "Lo", the Lord promises, "I am with you always to the close of the age" (Mt 28:20). I am with you. Amen!'

CHAPTER SIX

Baptism in the Spirit and the Universal Call to Holiness and Evangelisation

Echoing a point already made in chapter four, the Second Vatican Council stated that there were two universal calls to holiness and evangelisation which are shared by all baptised and confirmed Christians. Par. 1303 of the *CCC* explains: 'Confirmation brings an increase and deepening of baptismal grace.' This includes, 'a deeper level of intimacy with God the Father; closer union with Jesus; increase of the gifts of the Holy Spirit; a more perfect bond with the church; the special strength of the Holy Spirit to spread and defend the faith by word and action as true witnesses of Christ.' I would suggest that the holiness referred to is a matter of being filled, guided and empowered by the Spirit in daily life. (cf Eph 5:18; Gal 5:18; 5:25.) Evangelisation, as we saw in chapter one, is the task of bearing witness to Christ in word and deed in such a way that it leads to the conversion of individual lives and the transformation of cultural values and mores.

In par. 38 of his *Ecclesia in Oceania* Pope John Paul II pointed to the importance of the scriptures in holiness and evangelisation. 'The word of God in the Old and New Testaments is fundamental for all who believe in Christ and it is the inexhausible wellspring of evangelisation. Holiness of life and effective apostolic activity are born of constant listening to the word of God.' The Holy Father returned to this theme in pars 30-31 of *NMI*. This chapter will suggest that neither deep holiness or effective evangelisation is really possible without what Pentecostals and Charismatics refer to as 'baptism in the Spirit'. Due to the constraints of space I will not examine the scriptural understanding of this phenomenon. It has been ably dealt with in many books and articles.[1]

---

1. See, George T. Montague & Kilian McDonnell, *Christian Initiation and Baptism in the Holy Spirit* (Collegeville: The Liturgical Press, 1991), 3-80; Herbert Schneider, 'Baptism in the Spirit in the New Testament,' *The*

AN HISTORICALLY SIGNIFICANT EVENT

Those of us who are old enough to remember the Second Vatican Council can recall the great optimism there was when it concluded. We had wonderful blueprints for change in the liturgy, relationships with other Christian churches, and with the modern world. It was not long, however, when divisions and disillusionment set in. Thousands of priests and nuns left their vocations, and following the publication of *Humanae Vitae* which banned all forms of artificial contraception, millions of lay people dissented with papal authority. I can recall how two years prior to the contraception controversy, Fr Charles Davis, a well known British theologian, wrote perceptively in *America* on 29 January 1966: 'Much speaking in different places on themes of renewal has brought me into contact with many people seeking to revivify their faith. I have found a sense of emptiness, but together with it a deep yearning for God. There is an emptiness at the core of people's lives, an emptiness waiting to be filled. They are troubled about their faith; they find it slipping. I am not speaking of those who are worried about recent changes. These people are not. But they are looking for something more; they are looking for something to fill the void in their lives, and what they hear does not do that. The more perceptive know they are looking for God ... Who will speak to them quite simply of God as of a person he intimately knows, and make the reality and presence of God come alive for them once more?' Shortly after writing these words, Davis left the priesthood and the church.

On 17 February 1967, a few years after the conclusion of the Council, twenty-five students from Duquesne University attended a momentous retreat in The Ark and the Dove Retreat House on the outskirts of the city. Kevin and Dorothy Ranaghan have described their state of mind in this way: 'There was something lacking in their individual Christian lives. They couldn't quite put their finger on it, but somehow there was an emptiness, a lack of dynamism, a sapping of strength in their lives of

---

Holy Spirit and Power: The Catholic Charismatic Renewal, ed. Kilian McDonnell OSB (New York: Doubleday, 1975), 35-55; J. R. Williams, 'Baptism in the Holy Spirit,' *The New International Dictionary of the Pentecostal and Charismatic Movements*, eds, Stanley Burgess, Eduard van der Maas (Grand Rapids, Mi.: Zondervan, 2002), 354-363.

prayer and action. It was as if their lives as Christians were too much their own creation, as if they were moving forward under their own power and of their own will. It seemed to them that the Christian life wasn't meant to be a purely human achievement.' Each of the people who attended the retreat read David Wilkerson's *The Cross and the Switchblade*, the first four chapters of the Acts of the Apostles, and asked for a new outpouring of the Holy Spirit. Afterwards they claimed to have experienced a powerful release of the Spirit and his charismatic gifts.

Patti Mansfield has described her experience in these moving words: 'I wandered into the upstairs chapel ... not to pray but to tell any students there to come down to the [birthday] party. Yet, when I entered and knelt in the presence of Jesus in the Blessed Sacrament, I literally trembled with a sense of awe before his majesty. I knew in an overwhelming way that he is the King of Kings, the Lord of Lords. I thought, "You had better get out of here quick before something happens to you." But overriding my fear was a much greater desire to surrender myself unconditionally to God. I prayed, "Father, I give my life to you. Whatever you ask of me, I accept. And if it means suffering, I accept that too. Just teach me to follow Jesus and to love as he loves." In the next moment, I found myself prostrate, flat on my face, and flooded with an experience of the merciful love of God ... a love that is totally undeserved, yet lavishly given. Yes, it's true what St Paul writes: "The love of God has been poured into our hearts by the Holy Spirit." My shoes came off in the process. I was indeed on holy ground. I felt as if I wanted to die and be with God. The prayer of St Augustine captured my experience: "O Lord, you have made us for yourself and our hearts are restless until they rest in you." As much as I wanted to bask in his presence, I knew that if I, who am no one special, could experience the love of God in this way, that anyone across the face of the earth could do so.'[2]

This Pentecostal event fulfilled the promise implicit in the prophetic description of the nature and role of the charisms (1 Cor 12:8-10) in par. 12 of the *Dogmatic Constitution on the Church*, and par. 3 of the *Decree on the Apostolate of the Laity*. Since then, I

2. 'The Duquesne Weekend,' *Goodnews* Special Edition: 40 Years Catholic Charismatic Renewal (2007), 10-11.

myself, like over 100 million other Catholics all over the world, have been blessed to share the same experience.

A PERSONAL TESTIMONY

I was ordained in 1971. In the years immediately after that I had an inchoate longing for something. Twentieth century poet T. S. Eliot echoed that sentiment when he wrote in *Choruses from 'The Rock'*: 'the endless cycle of idea and action brings ... knowledge of words, and ignorance of the Word ... where is the wisdom we have lost in knowledge? Where is the knowledge we have lost in information?'[3] My head was stuffed with theology, statements about God, but I was out of touch with the Reality that those statements signified. I suspected that I was suffering from a famine of the experience of the Lord.

In February in 1974. I was invited to attend a retreat in the North of Ireland. One of the talks was given by a Church of Ireland clergyman. He spoke about Jesus as the source of our peace. Quite frankly, his inspired words moved me to tears. I wanted to know the Lord the way this man did. Afterwards a nun introduced me to him. We had a brief chat and arranged to meet privately. When we did, I told the clergyman that I was looking for a new awareness of God in my life. He read a memorable passage from Eph 3:16-20. It asks that the seeker, 'may have power, together with all the saints, to grasp how wide and long and high and deep is the love of Christ, and to know this love that surpasses knowledge – that you may be filled to the measure of all the fullness of God.' Then the clergyman prayed for me, firstly in English, then in tongues. Suddenly, and effortlessly, I too began to pray fluently in tongues. I knew with great conviction that Jesus loved me and accepted me as I was. I knew what St Peter meant when he wrote: 'Though you have not seen him, you love him and even though you do not see him now, you believe in him and are filled with an inexpressible and glorious joy' (1 Pet 1:8). May I say in passing that ever since that mystical event I have had a conviction that Baptism in the Spirit is, above all else, a movement from statements about God's unconditional love for each one of us, to a personal experience of the

---

3. *Selected Poems* (London: Faber & Faber, 1969), 107.

reality of that incomprehensible love. As William Barry has observed, 'If I do not know in my bones that God loves me with an everlasting love, I will not dare to open myself to his gaze and to seek to see myself as he sees me.'[4]

During the following months and years the inner effects were obvious. It was as if the risen Jesus had walked through the walls of my body to live within me (cf Gal 2:20). Prayer was easy, scripture a revelation, my fears were lessened, I had greater ability to love and exercise the spiritual gifts. Baptism in the Spirit, I discovered, is not so much a one-off blessing, as the beginning of a process, one that has been deepened and strengthened by subsequent in-fillings of the Holy Spirit over the years. As a result, it has strengthened my desire to be holy and to evangelise.

IS BAPTISM IN THE SPIRIT TRULY CATHOLIC?

I suspect that many Catholics are wary of the notion of baptism in the Spirit. Some admit, 'I do not even know what the phrase means,' others ask, 'if it is all that important, how come we never heard about it when we were growing up?' Still others wonder whether baptism in the Spirit is a Protestant notion, or a purely Pentecostal or Charismatic one. Here is a brief response to each objection.

The word baptism in English comes from Greek and means 'to immerse,' i.e. to soak, inundate, or saturate. In other words, to be baptised in the Spirit means to be filled with the Spirit (cf Eph 5:18). As John 1:33 shows, there is nothing new about the phrase 'baptised in the Spirit'. It is significant that Jesus used a similar phrase before his ascension into heaven when he said to the apostles, 'John baptised with water, but in a few days you will be baptised with the Holy Spirit' (Acts 1:5). While it is true that in modern times Charismatics have drawn attention to the importance of this blessing, it is necessary for every Catholic who wants to fulfill the church's universal call to holiness and evangelisation.

The Irish bishops referred to its ability to foster holiness

4. *Discernment in Prayer: Paying Attention to God* (Notre Dame: Ave Maria Press, 1990), 18.

when they said in par. 7 of a pastoral letter entitled *Life in the Spirit* that baptism in the Spirit is: 'The outpouring of the Holy Spirit is a conversion gift through which one receives a new and significant commitment to the Lordship of Jesus and openness to the power and gifts of the Holy Spirit. Perhaps only a minority of people experience this conversion as something sudden; for most people it seems it is more gradual, occurring over a period of days, weeks, or months.' Speaking about the infilling of the Spirit, the American bishops said a few years ago in a document entitled *Grace for a New Springtime*: 'The grace of baptism in the Holy Spirit is two-fold. It is first and foremost a coming to a living awareness of the true reality of Jesus Christ, as the Son of God.'[5] Unfortunately, although many Catholics believe that Jesus is the Son of God, and that he died for the forgiveness of sins, they do not have a deep personal relationship with him as the One who has dethroned their egos so as to reign at the very centre of their lives. When people are baptised in the Spirit, it is as if the risen Jesus has taken up residence within them. As a result of knowing in an experiential way that 'God has poured out his love into our hearts by the Holy Spirit, whom he has given us' (Rom 5:5), they have a new found desire to treat others the way they would like to be treated themselves, an increased ability to pray, a deeper insight into the spiritual meaning of the scriptures, a desire to be holy, and a growing urge to evangelise.

Secondly, the American bishops say that baptism in the Spirit results in 'an increased docility to the Holy Spirit and his power and gifts.' In par. 87 of *Mission of the Redeemer*, entitled, 'Being Led by the Spirit,' Pope John Paul II spoke on similar lines. The word docility in English comes from a Latin one which refers to a willingness to be taught inwardly by the Spirit. When people are filled by the Spirit, they move from being merely motivated by such things as laws, customs, duties, obligations and selfish impulses, to being inspired by the promptings of the Holy Spirit. When people are aware of being led in this way (cf Gal 5:18), they may feel that what they are being asked to do is beyond

---

5. In March 1997 the Administrative Committee of the National Conference of Catholic Bishops approved the publication of *Grace for the New Springtime* as a statement of the Ad Hoc Committee for Catholic Charismatic Renewal.

their natural power and ability. But as a result of baptism in the Spirit, they come to realise that God's power is made perfect in their weakness, and that they can do all things with the help of the One who strengthens them (Phil 4:13). As Paul observed, 'it is God who works in you (by his Spirit) to will and to act according to his good purpose' (Phil 2:13). Not only does the Spirit strengthen them in this way, when necessary he may give them supernatural gifts such as healing, miracle working and an ability to prophecy (cf 1 Cor 12:8-10).

BAPTISM IN THE SPIRIT IN THE LIVES OF THE SAINTS

When one reads the lives of the saints it becomes pretty obvious that many of them described religious awakenings that seemed to be similar to present day descriptions of baptism in the Spirit. I will briefly mention three out of many possible examples.

a) St Patrick

St Patrick (390-460), the apostle of Ireland, tells us that he was not gospel greedy as a teenager in Roman Britain. He wrote: 'I did not believe in the living God from my childhood.'[6] However, when he was brought to Ireland as a captive he experienced a crisis. In the midst of his afflictions he began to have a heartfelt desire for a revelation of God. Speaking about his subsequent religious awakening he said: 'I cannot hide the gift of God which he gave me in the land of my captivity. There I sought him and there I found him. The Lord made me aware of my unbelief that I might at last advert to my sins and turn wholeheartedly to the Lord my God.'[7] As a result of his conversion and religious awakening, Patrick says: 'More and more my faith grew stronger and my zeal so intense that in the course of a single day I would say as many as a hundred prayers, and almost as many at night.'[8] Time and time again in his *Confessions*, he mentioned how the Spirit guided and empowered him in ordinary and extraordinary ways.[9] Not only did he grow to be ex-

6. Maire de Paor, *Patrick the Pilgrim Apostle of Ireland: An Analysis of St Patrick's Confessio and Epistola* (Dublin: Veritas, 1998), 221.
7. Op. cit., 221.
8. Op. cit., 231
9. Pat Collins CM, 'Was St. Patrick a Charismatic?' *He Has Anointed Me* (Luton: New Life Publishing, 2005), 7-11.

ceptionally holy, he evangelised a nation. His description of his conversion and its lifelong effects seems to be a description of baptism in the Spirit and its effects.

b) St Louise de Marrilac

Louise de Marriliac (1591-1660), who founded the Daughters of Charity with St Vincent de Paul, once described a life-changing spiritual awakening she experienced during the celebration of the Eucharist, on Pentecost Sunday, 4 June 1623.[10] It is a striking fact that ever afterwards, she had an unusually strong devotion to the Holy Spirit. It would be no exaggeration to say that it lay at the heart of her spirituality. Over the years she often came back to the subject of the Spirit and the role it played in her life. For instance, she stated her intention of reflecting each morning on the role of the Holy Spirit in her own life. She wrote: 'Reflecting on my lowliness and powerlessness, I shall invoke the grace of the Holy Spirit in which I shall have great confidence for the accomplishment of his will in me, which shall be the sole desire of my heart.'[11] On another occasion she said: 'Let us pray that Our Lord Jesus Christ may bestow his Spirit upon us, so that we may be so filled with his Spirit that we may do nothing or say nothing except for his glory and his holy love ... O Eternal Light, lift my blindness! O Perfect Unity, create in me simplicity of being! Humble my heart to receive your graces. May the power of love which you have placed in my soul no longer stop at the disorder of my self-sufficiency which, in reality, is but powerlessness and an obstacle to the pure love which I must have as a result of the indwelling of the Holy Spirit.'[12] Not only did Louise grow in holiness, together with St Vincent de Paul she engaged in the evangelisation of the poor of her day.

c) St Thérèse of Lisieux

Thérèse of Lisieux (1873-1897) said in her autobiography that from the age of four to fifteen she was moody, oversensitive, immature, and inclined to cry a lot. Then at midnight Mass, on

---

10. *Spiritual Writings of Louise de Marillac: Correspondence and Thoughts* (New York: New City Press, 1991), 1.
11. Op. cit., 689.
12. Op. cit., 818.

Christmas Eve 1886, she had a life-changing religious experience. She called it her night of conversion and illumination. 'Charity had found its way into my heart,' she declares, 'calling on me to forget myself and simply do what God wanted of me.'[13] I feel confident in saying that Thérèse had experienced what Pentecostals and Charismatics refer to as baptism in the Spirit.[14] Afterwards, she said that as a result of this spiritual awakening: 'I felt a great desire to work for the conversion of sinners.'[15] It is significant that besides being canonised she was designated a patroness of the missions because of her zeal for souls.

Although there are similarities in the way people recount their experiences of baptism in the Spirit, there are many individual differences, e.g. for some it is sudden and dramatic, for others it is more gradual and gentle. Furthermore, when theologians reflect on such experiences they adopt different approaches, e.g. baptism in the Spirit is the release of a grace already given in baptism and confirmation, or a new outpouring or effusion of the Spirit. They can also emphasise different scriptural and historical points. As a result, there are different ways of understanding baptism in the Spirit and how it fits into the more general context of the sacramental and missionary life of the church.

As Frank D. Macchia indicates in his excellent *Baptized in the Spirit: A Global Pentecostal Theology*, the Pentecostals were the first Christians in the modern era to talk about baptism in the Spirit. They described two blessings, firstly, salvation and sanctification as a result of water baptism, and secondly, power to witness to one's faith, together with charismatic signs, especially tongues, as a result of baptism in the Spirit.[16] James Dunn pointed out in his book *Baptism in the Holy Spirit*, that while Catholic and Protestant scholars would not doubt the genuineness of Pentecostals' experience of the Spirit, they would question the

---

13. *Autobiography of a Saint*, (London: Harvill Press, 1958), 128
14. Pat Collins CM, 'Therese of Lisieux: A Saint for Our Times,' *The Broken Image* (Dublin: Columba, 2002), 175-195.
15. *Autobiography of a Saint*, op. cit., 128
16. (Grand Rapids: Zondervan, 2006), 28-38

way they interpret it from a scriptural and theological point of view.[17]

The writings of eminent Catholic scholars such as Frs Yves Congar,[18] Frank Sullivan, Raniero Cantalamessa,[19] Killian Mc Donnell, and George Montague indicate that there are two main ways of understanding baptism in the Spirit. Firstly, many of these scholars maintain that baptism in the Spirit is the conscious release, manifestation, and appropriation of dormant graces already received in the sacraments of baptism and confirmation. This thesis was first proposed in Cardinal Suenens's *Theological and Pastoral Orientations of the Catholic Charismatic Renewal*.[20] It has been adopted and developed by many theologians since then. Mc Donnell and Montague indicated in their book *Christian Initiation and Baptism in the Holy Spirit: Evidence from the First Eight Centuries* that when adults were being baptised in the early church they expected to be baptised in the Spirit and to receive one or more of the charisms. They cite the fact that doctors of the church, Hilary of Poitiers, Cyril of Jerusalem and John Chrysostom bore united testimony to the fact that baptism in the Holy Spirit was not a matter of private piety, but rather an aspect of the sacred liturgy, and of the church's public life. They concluded that this special grace is integral to the sacraments of initiation and *normative* for all Christians. They write: 'Because it belongs to the church as an integral element of Christian initiation, it must be taken with utter seriousness. Indeed the baptism in the Spirit is normative.'[21] If their interpretation of the scriptural and patristic data is correct, their conclusion has vital implications for the renewal of the contemporary church. For example, many Catholics believe that as adults we need to appropriate in a conscious way, the graces we first received in a sacramental manner in baptism and confirmation. This happens as a result of claiming those

---

17. (London: SCM Press, 1970),
18. 'Baptism in the Spirit', *I Believe in the Holy Spirit: The Complete Three Volume Work in One Volume* (New York: Crossroad/Herder, 2000), vol II, 189-201.
19. 'Baptism in the Spirit,' *Charisindia* (Sept. 2005), 8-12.
20. (Notre Dame: Word of Life, 1974), 30-33.
21. Op. cit., 337.

sacramental graces by means of personal faith. Otherwise they tend to remain inactive rather than active in our lives. In par. 51 of his letter, *Lord and Giver of Life* (1986), Pope John Paul II explained, 'faith, in its deepest essence, is the openness of the human heart to the gift of God's self- communication in the Holy Spirit.'

Frank Sullivan SJ published an influential article in *Gregorianum*, entitled, 'Baptism in the Holy Spirit'. Speaking of this grace he said that it was 'a religious experience which initiates a decisively new sense of the powerful presence and working of God in one's life, which working usually involves one or more charismatic gifts.'[22] It is interesting to note that Karl Rahner also saw baptism in the Spirit as a religious experience. He wrote: 'We cannot doubt that in this life we can experience grace in such a way that it gives us a sense of freedom and opens up horizons that are entirely new, making a profound impression on us, transforming and molding in us, even over a long period of time, a more inward Christian attitude. There is nothing that prevents us calling that kind of experience a baptism in the Spirit.'[23] While not denying that, ultimately, all Christian grace has its origin in the sacraments of initiation, Sullivan said that St Thomas taught in the *Summa Theologica*, I, q, 43, a.6, ad 2 that when people experience an infilling or effusion of the Spirit, such as baptism in the Spirit, God lives in them in a new way, in order that they might do a new thing, such as working miracles, prophesying, or offering their lives as martyrs. In this understanding, baptism in the Spirit is not so much a one-off event, but rather the initiation of an on-going process that allows for new in-fillings of the Spirit which deepen and strengthen the life of grace and witness.[24]

There is reason to believe that the two views of baptism in the Spirit are complementary rather than contradictory. This religious experience is rooted in the graces received in the sacraments of initiation, but besides releasing their potential, there is

22. *Gregorianum* 55, (1974), 4.
23. *Erfahrung des Heiligen Geistes*, in *Schrifen zur Theologie*, vol 13 (Zurich: Einsiedeln-Koln, 1978), 232.
24. *Charisms and Charismatic Renewal: A Biblical and Theological Study* (Dublin: Gill & Macmillan, 1982), 70-75.

reason to think that something new, such as the charisms listed in 1 Cor 12:8-10 is added. It has often struck me that when Jesus was baptised in the Spirit in the Jordan, and the apostles and the disciples were inundated by the Holy Spirit in the upper room, not only did they experience the love of God being poured into their hearts (cf Rom 5:5), they were also empowered and gifted to witness to that love. Whereas Jesus did not seem to have preached or performed any deeds of power before his baptism, he did so continuously afterwards. It was the same with the first Christians. Following Pentecost they began to proclaim the reign of God's liberating mercy and to demonstrate its presence by means of the more remarkable charisms, such as healing and miracle working.

Fr Peter Hocken has made it clear in a number of his writings, most recently in two *Goodnews* articles entitled 'Baptism in the Spirit: A Biblical Understanding' (Sept/Oct 2007, 20-23) and 'Baptism in the Spirit: A Catholic Approach' (Nov/Dec 2007, 10-11), that he is not impressed by either of the approaches outlined above. He feels that they are not sufficiently rooted in scripture. He maintains that the coming of the Spirit at Pentecost, and *ipso facto* all subsequent sendings, have an eschatological dimension in so far as they are an anticipation of the second coming of Jesus at the end of time. He has written: 'The implication of the biblical data is that Jesus has come to baptise in the Holy Spirit. This he begins to do after his resurrection and ascension. This immersion in the Holy Spirit is to prepare the way for the coming King and his rule in righteousness. In this light, we should understand the outpouring of the 20th century as a sign of the Lord's coming in glory. That does not mean we have any idea of God's precise timetable.'

It could be added by way of addendum that baptism in the Spirit could be considered as a sacramental like exorcism (cf *CCC* par. 1673). In par. 1677 of the *Catechism* we read: 'Sacramentals are sacred signs instituted by the church. They prepare men to receive the fruit of the sacraments and sanctify different circumstances of life.' Par. 1670 explains: 'Sacramentals do not confer the grace of the Holy Spirit in the way that the sacraments do ... For well-disposed members of the faithful, the liturgy of the sacraments and sacramentals sanctifies almost every event of their lives with the divine grace which flows from the Paschal mystery of the passion, death, and resurrection of Christ. From this source all sacraments and sacramentals draw their power.' Arguably, when believers lay hands on people, or anoint them with blessed oil, while praying that they be filled with the Spirit, it is a sacramental, and is thus related to sacramental grace.

HOW TO RECEIVE THE BAPTISM IN THE HOLY SPIRIT

How does a person become baptised in the Holy Spirit? In my experience, four things are necessary. Firstly, he or she needs a wholehearted desire for this grace. Sometimes it takes months and even years for the desire to deepen and strengthen to such a point that the personality is sufficiently open to receive the unmerited gift of the outpouring of the Spirit. Allied to this is the importance of removing obstacles to the Spirit's coming. We can pray with the Psalmist, 'Search me, O God, and know my heart; test me and know my anxious thoughts. See if there is any offensive way in me' Ps 139:23-24.

Secondly, it is important to rely on the infallible promises of God to send the Spirit to those whose desire prompts them to ask for it. Here is just one of many possible New Testament examples. In Lk 11:13, Jesus said to parents, 'If you then, though you are evil, know how to give good gifts to your children, how much more will your Father in heaven give the Holy Spirit to those who ask him!' As Catholics, we pray to Mary, the mother of Jesus, to be worthy of this mighty promise of Christ.

Thirdly, it is important that those who desire to be filled with the Spirit would be willing to turn away from any obstacle that might stand in the way. While all unrepented sin is a barrier, in my experience the greatest single obstacle is resentment, an unwillingness to forgive past hurts and injustices whether real or imaginary. Incidentally, scripture seems to confirm that impression, for example in Mk 11:24-25; Lk 6:36-38. So it is necessary for those who want to be baptised in the Spirit to prepare by being willing, with God's help, to turn away from sin, especially the sin of anger and antagonism against any person living or dead.

Fourthly, people should ask to be baptised in the Spirit with real expectancy. There are many gifts we could ask of God, without being certain that they were in accord with the divine will. But to ask to be filled with the Holy Spirit is always in accord with the centrality of God's will. As scripture assures us: 'This is the confidence we have in approaching God: that if we ask anything according to his will, he hears us. And if we know that he hears us – whatever we ask – we know that we have what we asked of him' (1 Jn 5:14-15). As soon as people begin to ask for the sending of the Spirit, they receive a first installment of that grace. At the outset they may not be consciously aware of any inner change. But then, either suddenly or gradually, their relationship with Christ will deepen as a result of a religious awakening and thus become more intimate at a conscious level of awareness.

If you want to pray for an in-filling of the Holy Spirit, begin by answering these questions: 'Do you believe that Jesus is the Son of God, that he died to free us from our sins and was raised from the dead to bring us new life? Will you follow Jesus as your Lord?' When you make your profession of faith, say the following prayer with sincerity of heart and expectant trust: 'Lord Jesus Christ, I want to belong more fully to you from this time forward. I want to be freed from the power of sin and the evil one. I want to enter more completely into your kingdom to be part of your people. I will turn away from all wrongdoing, and I will avoid everything that leads me to wrongdoing. I ask you to forgive all the sins that I have committed. I offer my life to you, and I promise to put you first in my life and to seek to do your will. I ask you now to drench, soak, and inundate me with your Holy Spirit. I believe that your spiritual hands are upon me and that the red light of your mercy and the white light of your love are flooding my body, mind and soul. I thank you, Lord, that even as I pray you are responding to my request because it is so in accord with your loving desire for me. Amen.'

BAPTISM IN THE SPIRIT AND THE GIFTS OF THE SPIRIT

It is a striking fact, as I mentioned already, that Jesus only began to exercise the gifts of the Spirit after his baptism in the Jordan when he was anointed by the Holy Spirit. It was much the same for the apostles, as soon as they were empowered by the promised Holy Spirit at Pentecost they began to exercise the charismatic gifts. Echoing the teaching of the Second Vatican Council, par. 24 of the apostolic exhortation, *On The Vocation and the Mission of the Lay Faithful in the Church and in the World*, says: 'Whether they be exceptional and great or simple and ordinary, the charisms are graces of the Holy Spirit that have, directly or indirectly, a usefulness for the ecclesial community, ordered as they are to the building up of the church, to the well-being of humanity and to the needs of the world ... The charisms are received in gratitude both on the part of the one who receives them, and also on the part of the entire church. They are in fact a singularly rich source of grace for the vitality of the apostolate.' But as scripture and contemporary experience seem to attest, the gifts are not released in people's lives until they are baptised in the Holy Spirit. So it seems to me that the bishop, priest, religious or lay person who has not been filled with the Spirit and his gifts, will be unable to carry out the universal call to the new evangelisation as effectively as would otherwise be possible.

BAPTISM IN THE SPIRIT AND HOLINESS

All of us are called to holiness. As Jesus said, 'Be perfect as your heavenly Father is perfect' (Mt 5:48). There are different ways of describing what holiness is. One way of doing so is to say that it is a matter of being filled, guided and empowered by the Spirit of God. When people are baptised in the Spirit, they experience that infilling 'because God has poured out his love into our hearts by the Holy Spirit, whom he has given us' (Rom 5:5). As a result they can say with utter conviction, 'I live by faith in the Son of God, who loved me and gave himself for me' (Gal 2:20). The Spirit of Jesus impels them to turn away from anything that would be incompatible with that divine love while urging them to express it to both God and people in a credible way.

People who have experienced the effusion of the Holy Spirit find that they are guided by the Spirit (Gal 5:18) in all sorts of ways, e.g. the whispers of conscience, inner promptings, words of knowledge, scriptural inspirations, etc. When they get such inspirations, they rely upon the action of the Holy Spirit within them to empower them to do God's will even if it seems beyond the limitations of their human nature. As par. 521 of the *CCC* points out, 'Christ enables us to live in him all that he himself lived, and he lives it in us.' There is an anomaly involved here. When people are baptised in the Spirit that they may find that they can exercise the extraordinary gifts of the Spirit such as those listed by St Paul in 1 Cor 12:8-10. As was noted in chapters three and four, a number of theologians, notably Thomas Aquinas, state that the exercise of the gifts *gratis datae* is not necessarily a sign of holiness, because although a person may have been baptised in the Spirit he or she may have fallen out of the state of sanctifying grace as a result of serious sin and yet continued to exercise the gifts. However, in my experience baptism in the Spirit not only makes the exercise of those gifts possible, it usually tends to move the person toward greater holiness of life, e.g. by means of heartfelt prayer and growing union with God.

BAPTISM IN THE SPIRIT AND THE EUCHARIST

Some time ago, on the feast of Christ's baptism, I had an unusual awareness as I celebrated Mass. During the Eucharistic Prayer, I was thinking of how the Spirit would come down during the words of consecration to transform the bread and wine into the body, blood, soul and divinity of Jesus Christ. Then, I prayed inwardly, 'Lord, as you send the Spirit upon the gifts, send it also upon me and the congregation.' As I said this, I had a conviction that God was responding. By the time I got to the words of consecration I was so moved with emotion that I could hardly speak. I had a profound sense of the link between the baptism of Jesus in the Jordan and his saving death on the cross. On the day he was revealed to the world as God's anointed Messiah, there was an intimation of the agonies to come for God's suffering servant (cf Is 42:1). Jesus fulfilled that vocation when he willingly laid down his life for all mankind (cf Rom 5:6-8). When he could breathe no longer, he gave a loud cry and said, 'Father into our hands I *commit my spirit* [my italics]' (Lk 23:46). So at the very moment of his death, Jesus yielded up the breath of the Holy Spirit so that it could be given to all of us. As I blessed the bread and wine I had a heartfelt sense that the same Spirit was coming, simultaneously, upon the gifts, the congregation, and myself in a transforming way. So whenever we celebrate the Eucharist, all of us can earnestly ask, in the words of the third Eucharistic

Prayer, 'Grant that we who are nourished by his body and blood, may be filled with his Holy Spirit.'

THE SACRAMENTS OF INITIATION

Authors George Montague and Kilian Mc Donnell maintained in their book, *Christian Initiation and Baptism in the Holy Spirit: Evidence from the First Eight Centuries,*[25] that in the early years of Christian history, those who received the sacraments of initiation expected to be baptised in the Spirit and to receive the charisms. How many contemporary clergy or their congregations expect the Spirit to be poured out in such power, e.g. when the sacraments of initiation are administered at the Easter Vigil? For example, it should not be uncommon for some of the recipients to praise God in tongues or utter prophetic words. It is important that all involved with preparatory catechesis should urge candidates to be open to the possibility of receiving these or other manifestations of the Spirit's presence and activity. Normally the charisms of the Spirit are not mentioned during RCIA courses.

At a conferring of the sacrament of confirmation which I attended in Michigan, the bishop failed to mention the name of Jesus, the New Testament charisms, or the link between the sacrament and evangelisation. Unfortunately this is not an uncommon occurrence.[26] Is it any wonder, then, that confirmation seems to be a rite of passage out of the church rather than a commission that empowers its recipients to be effective witnesses for Christ? Confirmation, as the *CCC* says in par. 1303, 'increases the gifts of the Spirit within us,' and 'gives us a special strength of the Holy Spirit to spread and defend the faith by word and action as true witnesses of Christ.' When children or adults are being prepared for the sacrament of confirmation they need to be told not only about the Old Testament gifts of the Spirit listed in Is 11:2, but also about the New Testament charisms listed in 1

25. (Collegeville: Liturgical Press, 1991).
26. It is really surprising, not to say disappointing, to find that in his book entitled, *Charisms and the New Evangelisation* (Middlegreen, Slough: St Paul Publications, 1992), Bishop Paul Joseph Cordes never seems to mention either baptism in the Spirit or the charisms listed by St Paul in 1 Cor 12:8-10.

Cor 12:8-10 and elsewhere in the New Testament. They can also be told how the special charisms can equip their recipients to witness effectively to the person and teachings of Jesus Christ.

CONCLUSION

This chapter began by suggesting that holiness and evangelisation are intimately interlinked. While it is true that baptism in the Spirit has been rediscovered by the Pentecostal and Charismatic movements, it has always been a gift for all the church. As the booklet *Fanning the Flame* observes: 'Accepting the baptism in the Spirit is not joining a movement, any movement.'[27] In another place McDonnell and Montague add: 'It is not – as viewed by many today – an optional spirituality in the church such as ... the devotion to the Sacred Heart or the stations of the cross. The baptism in the Holy Spirit does not belong to private piety ... *it is the spirituality of the church* (my italics).'[28] Because it is so clearly associated with the sacraments of initiation, a concerted effort is needed, when preparing candidates for baptism and confirmation, to be open, as mentioned already, to the possibility of receiving one or more of the gifts of the Spirit Catholics will be enabled by means of the new evangelisation to bring about the new springtime, spoken about by Pope John Paul II, in par. 86 of *Mission of the Redeemer*. 'God is preparing a great springtime, for Christianity,' he observed, 'and we can already see its first signs.' There is an obvious need to integrate this notion into everyday Catholic spirituality, at every level of the church, in the conviction that the fullness of the Spirit is indispensable if one hopes to respond effectively to the universal calls to holiness and evangelisation. As was noted elsewhere, the Life in the Spirit Seminars and the Holy Spirit weekends on Alpha courses are designed to help people to receive the infilling of the Spirit.

---

27. Eds, Kilian McDonnell and George Montague (Collegeville: The Liturgical Press, 1991), 21.
28. *Christian Initiation and the Baptism in the Holy Spirit*, op. cit., 337.

CHAPTER SEVEN

Charisms and the New Evangelisation: Some Contemporary Examples

This chapter focuses attention on the so called 'third wave' in renewal, which highlights the role of signs and wonders in evangelisation. That will be followed by a brief examination of the connection between charisms, especially those of power, in three Catholic evangelistic groups: Alpha, Parish Cells, and Harvesters.

The Third Wave

Peter Wagner, a former professor of Church Growth at Fuller Theological Seminary in Pasadena, California, was the first person to coin the term 'Third Wave' which has been widely adopted since. In the 1980s it referred to a phase of renewal in the Holy Spirit that followed from the first Pentecostal wave and the second Charismatic wave. Although the third wave emphasised such things as exorcism, healing and the working of miracles, in theory it was not associated with either Pentecostalism or the Charismatic Movement. In actual fact, however, not only did the third wave have strong affinities with the theology of its predecessors, its message exercised quite an influence in the Protestant and Catholic wings of the Charismatic Movement, especially in English-speaking countries.

John Wimber (1934-1997), who later became the founder of The Vineyard Christian Fellowship, was probably the most influential person as far as the third wave was concerned. His views about evangelisation were influenced by the remarkable ministries of Smith Wigglesworth (1859-1947) in Britain,[1] and

---

1. Jack Hywel-Davies, *Baptism by Fire: Story of Smith Wigglesworth* (London: Hodder Christian Paperbacks, 1987); Smith Wigglesworth, *Greater Works: Experiencing God's Power* (New Kensington, PA.: Whitaker House, 2000) This is an anthology of a number of his writings. See Pat Collins CM, 'Intimations of Unity' *Goodnews* (May/June 2006), 14-15.

Kathryn Kuhlman (1907-1976)[2] in the United States. In 1981 he delivered a lecture at Fuller Theological Seminary entitled, 'Signs, Wonders and Church Growth.' Then, from 1982 to 1985 he taught the very popular MC510 course at the seminary, entitled 'The Miraculous and Church Growth.' Although 2,800 students enrolled, it was discontinued after four years as a result of the controversy it stirred up. However, Wimber continued to speak about the role of signs and wonders in power evangelism in America. He also lectured abroad, e.g. in Britain and Ireland. In 1986 his Fuller lecture notes were edited by Kevin Springer and published with the title, *Power Evangelism*.[3] Not surprisingly, Wimber saw Jesus as the archetypal evangeliser whose main message was the proclamation of the coming of the kingdom of God.[4] Wimber highlighted seven main signs of its advent.[5]

The first was, and still is, Jesus himself in the midst of his people (Lk 17:21; Mt 18:20), whose presence brings joy, peace, and a sense of celebration (Jn 5:11; 16:33; Mk 2:18-20).

The second sign is the preaching of the gospel. There was no gospel of the kingdom to proclaim until Christ arrived. Now that he has come, however, the good news of the kingdom must be preached to all, especially to the poor (Lk 4:18-19; 7:22).[6] The preaching of the kingdom points people to Christ.

The third sign of the kingdom is exorcism. Evil powers are expelled. Wimber, who was well aware of the secularising, anti-supernatural tendencies of post-Enlightenment Western culture,

---

2. Jamie Buckingham, *Daughter of Destiny: Kathryn Kuhlman Her Story* (Plainfield, New Jersey: Logos International, 1978); Kathryn Kulhman, *I Believe in Miracles* (London: Lakeland, 1974); Pat Collins CM, 'Modern Charismatics and the Charism of Expectant Faith,' in *Expectant Faith* (Dublin: Columba, 1997).
3. (San Francisco: Harper & Row, 1986).
4. Wimber's theology of the kingdom was very much influenced by George Eldon Ladd's, *Jesus and the Kingdom* (New York: Harper & Row, 1964).
5. Summary at John Wimber *Power Evangelism* http://www.pastornet.net.au/renewal/journal10/b-wimber.html (accessed 9 April, 2008).
6. St Vincent de Paul thought that this was *the* evangelical sign of the coming of the kingdom, even more important than signs and wonders (Lk 7:22). As a result, his most characteristic way of referring to Jesus was, 'the Evangeliser of the poor.'

was influenced by Harry Blamire's classic book, *The Christian Mind*.[7] It argues that Christians see everything *sub specie aeternitatis* and believe in the possibility of supernatural interventions in this world. He was also influenced by the writing of one of his colleagues in Fuller, Dr Paul Hiebert. He argued that while many Westerners believed in the empirical and the transcendent worlds, because of their adherence to the notion of a closed world ruled by the inexorable laws of causality, they tended to rule out the possibility of an in-between realm where supernatural forces could be at work. Wimber refused to demythologise the teachings of Jesus and his apostles about demons. Although the 'principalities and powers' may refer to demonic ideologies and structures, he believed that they can also refer to evil, personal intelligences under the command of the devil. Demonic influence and possession is a real and terrible condition. Deliverance is only possible in and through, what he referred to as, a 'power encounter' in which the name of Jesus is invoked and seen to prevail.

The fourth sign of the Kingdom, according to Wimber, was the healing of people, e.g., making the blind see, the deaf hear, the lame walk, the sick whole, raising the dead, and nature miracles, e.g. stilling the storm, and multiplying the loaves and fishes. These deeds of power were not only signs pointing to the reality of the kingdom's arrival, but also anticipations of the final and definitive coming of the eschatological kingdom when all disease, hunger, disorder, and death will be banished forever. God, he said, is still free and powerful by performing miracles, especially in frontier situations where the kingdom is advancing into enemy-held territory. He noted the fact that some people, such as himself, thought that they should expect miracles as commonly as in the ministry of Jesus and his apostles (Jn 14:12). He acknowledged that there were others, mainly cessationists, who drew attention to the texts which describe these miracles as authenticating only the unique ministry of the founders of Christianity (Heb 2:3-4; 2 Cor 12:12).

A fifth sign of the Kingdom is the graced phenomenon of conversion and new birth in the Spirit. Whenever people 'turn to God from idols, to serve the living and true God' (1 Thess 1:9,

---

7. (Ann Arbor, MI: Servant Books, 1978), 67-85.

10), a power encounter takes place in which the influence of idols and associated spirits, whether traditional or modern, is broken. As a result, God's power of salvation is displayed (Rom 1:16), and converts who have been rescued from Satan and darkness are brought into the light and the power of God (Acts 26:18) are said to have 'tasted ... the powers of the age to come' (Heb 6:5).

A sixth sign of the kingdom are the Christian people of the kingdom in whom Christ-like qualities are manifested, such as those which were referred to by Paul as 'the fruit of the Spirit' (Gal 5:16). The gift of the Spirit is the supreme blessing of the kingdom of God and where the Spirit rules, love, joy, peace, and righteousness rule with him (Rom 14:17). Furthermore, love issues in good works. Thus, if the gospel is good news of the kingdom, good works are signs of the kingdom. Good news and good works, evangelism and social responsibility once again are seen to be indissolubly united. John Wimber's wife, Carol, was raised a Catholic, and the couple were married in a Catholic ceremony. It is not all that surprising, therefore, that Wimber, a Quaker, and a committed ecumenist, seemed to reflect a Catholic understanding of justification.

The seventh sign of the kingdom, is suffering. It was necessary for the King to suffer in order to enter into his glory. He suffered for us, leaving us an example that we should follow in his steps (1 Pet 2:21). To suffer for the sake of righteousness or as a result of our witness to Jesus, and to bear such suffering with courage, is a clear sign to all who see it, that faithful Christians have received God's salvation and kingdom (Phil 1:28-29; 2 Thess 1:5).

There were a number of distinctive features in Wimber's understanding of evangelisation which are worth mentioning. Firstly, he made a distinction between programmatic and power evangelisation. Speaking about the former he said: 'Programmatic evangelism attempts to reach minds and hearts of people without the aid of charismatic gifts.'[8] He went on to say that, typically, it does this by means of efficient organisation and rational preaching to passive congregations in the belief that if people

---

8. Wimber, *Power Evangelism*, 45.

are persuaded of the truth they will embrace it in a life-trans-
forming way. Anyone familiar with Catholic parish missions
would recognise what Wimber was describing. While not necessarily being against programmatic evangelisation, Wimber felt
that it needed to be augmented with power evangelisation.
Here, 'each evangelism experience is initiated by the Holy Spirit
for a specific place, time, person or group ... in power evangelism, Christians are consciously under God's commission and
control.'[9] Echoing Peter Wagner, Wimber also made a distinction between presence, proclamation, and persuasive evangelisation. The first seeks to convert people solely by means of the
example of a life well lived, e.g. by performing works of mercy.
The second focuses on a didactic approach, e.g. by means of
teaching and preaching. The third seeks to move a person from a
decision to accept Christ as one's Saviour, to faithful, intentional
discipleship.

Wimber maintained that divine appointments were providential opportunities for evangelisation. 'A divine appointment,'
he explained, 'is an appointed time in which God reveals himself to an individual or group through spiritual gifts or other
supernatural phenomena ... they are meetings he has ordained
to demonstrate his kingdom (Eph 2:10).'[10] He cited the story of
the encounter between Philip and the Ethiopian eunuch in Acts
8:26-40 as a good example of what he had in mind. Throughout
that divine appointment in the wilderness, Philip was guided by
means of the Spirit and his gifts. Wimber also talked about
power encounters. Evangelists are often confronted by great
need. From a human point of view they feel powerless, e.g. to
convert someone, drive out an evil spirit, or heal an illness. But
God's power is made perfect in human weakness (2 Cor 12:9);
the evangelist can do all things with the help of the One who
strengthens him or her (Phil 4:13). When the evangelist relies on
the fact that God is at work within his or her heart, a power encounter takes place in such a way that there is an in-breaking of
the liberating presence of God's kingdom. Wimber's emphasis
on the activity of the Spirit in the evangelised and the evangelis-

9. Ibid., 46.
10. Ibid., 51.

ers would seem to conform to the views of Paul VI as expressed in *EN* par. 75 and John Paul II in *RM* par. 21.

There is a reciprocal relationship between objective scriptural and ecclesiastical truth and subjective religious experience. However, the genuineness of experience needs to be discerned in the light of dogmatic truth. Arguably, John Wimber placed too much reliance on his own religious experience. He seemed to take it as normative and to use it as a reliable hermeneutic when interpreting the scriptures. However, it could be argued that although he was a good man, he was not a good exegete and that some of his scriptural interpretations were naïve and even fundamentalist. When his course was cancelled at Fuller, a report entitled *Ministry and the Miraculous, A Case Study at Fuller Theological Seminary* was edited by Lewis Smedes. It seemed to make a similar point. 'Jesus' instructions to his disciples to prepare his way for the lost sheep of the house of Israel are not the same as his instructions to his universal church ... the church at large was not commissioned to heal the sick and raise the dead, and ... when Jesus sent his disciples on a special mission to heal the sick and raise the dead (Mt 10; Lk 10), he did not commission the church to do the same.'[11]

While performance of signs and wonders is not a necessary concomitant of evangelisation it is a possible one, as the remarkable deeds of the saints down the ages testifies. This balance was well expressed in par. 12 of *De Ecclesia* when it said on the one hand that 'charisms ... are to be received with thanksgiving and consolation,' while on the other, 'extraordinary gifts are not to be rashly sought after, nor are the fruits of apostolic labour to be presumptuously expected from their use.'

THE SPIRIT, CHARISMS AND EVANGELISATION
IN THREE CATHOLIC GROUPS

Although the so-called third wave tried to separate from the two previous waves of renewal, it was not very successful in doing so at a practical level. Apart from not praying in tongues, there was little difference between them from a general theological

---

11. *Ministry and the Miraculous, A Case Study at Fuller Theological Seminary* (Pasadena, CA: Fuller Theological Seminary, 1987), 30.

point of view. Other evangelistic movements, of a 'third wave' kind, have emerged within the Protestant and Catholic charismatic 'second wave.' The link between charisms and evangelisation in three Catholic groups will be briefly instanced here, i.e. Alpha, Parish Cells, and Harvesters.

a) Alpha

Commenting on Alpha in his interesting book, *God's Continent: Christianity, Islam and Europe's Religious Crisis,* Professor Philip Jenkins says: 'The Alpha course is designed for a society in which Christians possess minority status and can assume no wide knowledge whatever of their doctrines or beliefs. With its assumptions of individualism, popular skepticism, and non-hierarchical networking and its unwillingness to invoke dogmatic authority it is intended to confront the forces driving toward secularisation and to use those forces for evangelistic ends.'[12]

Alpha started off as a ten-week introduction to the Christian faith that included fifteen talks. They are available in Nicky Gumbel's *Alpha: Questions of Life*. While they originated from within a Charismatic parish they are intentionally not associated with the Charismatic Movement in order that they may be more acceptable to the general public. The topics covered include: 'Christianity: boring, untrue and irrelevant?' 'Who is Jesus?' 'Why did Jesus die?' 'Who is the Holy Spirit?' and 'Why and how should I read the Bible?' It is important to stress the fact that the Alpha course is designed primarily to meet the needs of unbelievers and lapsed people. It has been adapted for use by Catholics (Catholic Alpha), and has received the approval of bishops in countries such as England, France and Ireland. While it is true that the first few Alpha courses will usually be attended by people who do practise their faith, they only become truly effective from an evangelistic point of view, to the extent that those first participants invite non-practising relatives, friends and colleagues to attend subsequent courses. The kerygmatic talks presume nothing and appeal to mind and heart. They try to persuade the listeners without pressurising them in any way. In

---

12. (Oxford: Oxford University Press, 2007), 83.

recent years a number of new Alpha courses have been developed.[13]

Because it originated in a Charismatic parish, the Alpha course emphasises the importance of baptism in the Spirit, evangelisation and openness to the gifts of the Spirit. Around the middle of the course, the participants go away for either a day or a weekend. During that time they hear and discuss a number of talks on the Holy Spirit. They can be prayed with for an infilling of the Spirit. Many of those attending opt for this. It usually marks their passage from curiosity about Christianity to personal commitment to Christ. When one listens to the participants describing their experiences it becomes evident that a number of them are baptised in the Spirit. Some of them speak in tongues though this gift is not highlighted too much in the talks. Later in the course there is a session devoted to the question, 'Why and how should I tell others?'[14] It stresses the fundamental importance of evangelisation in the Christian life by means of such things as personal witness, persuasion, proclamation, prayer and power. Speaking of the latter it says, 'In the New Testament the proclamation of the gospel is often accompanied by a demonstration of the power of God ... Proclamation and demonstration go hand in hand. Often one leads to the other.'[15]

It cites the account of Peter curing the cripple at the temple gate in Acts 3:1-10 as a biblical example. In the following session entitled, 'Does God Heal Today?' the issue of God's supernatural intervention in our lives by means of deeds of power is discussed.[16] It answers in the affirmative and says among other things: 'God is still healing people today. There are so many wonderful stories of God healing that it is difficult to know which to give as an example.'[17] One of the notable characteristics of Alpha conferences is the level of expectant faith that is evident. It reminded me of Wimber's notion of power encounters. In

---

13. They include Student Alpha; Youth Alpha Alpha in the workplace; Senior Alpha; Alpha for Prisons; The Alpha Marriage Course; Deaf Alpha.
14. Gumbel, *Alpha: Questions of Life*, 171-86.
15. Ibid., 182-183.
16. Ibid., 187-202.
17. Ibid., 197.

fact it seems quite clear that Nicky Gumbel's approach in Alpha was much influenced by John Wimber. The two men met during one of the American's visits to England in the 1980s. It is estimated that, to date, about eleven million people have attended Alpha courses in countries around the world including two million in Britain where about 80% of the population is unchurched.

b) Parish Cells

Parish cells were first developed by the Protestant minister, Dr Paul Yonggi Cho in Korea. Some years later Mgr Michael Ivers of St Boniface parish in Pembroke Pines in Florida adapted the Korean model. In the mid 1980s Dom Pigi Perini, of St Estorgio parish in central Milan, was looking for something that might revitalise his dying parish where only 5% of the people were practising. He visited St Boniface parish and afterwards adopted and adapted the Florida version of the cell groups.[18] Don Perini says that as a result of his visit to the US he underwent a fundamental change of mind. He moved from a maintenance model of parish to a missionary one and took to heart Paul VI's dictum that 'The church exists to evangelise.'[19] He introduced the cells into his parish in 1986. As a result, St Eustorgio has been transformed over the last twenty years. Currently there are 120 groups with about ten people in each. They meet once a week and are sometimes referred to as an evangelising cells or *Oikos*, a Greek word that refers to a group with ties of family, work, friendship, common interests etc. The group meetings consist of seven key elements: song and praise, sharing, teaching, discussion, business, intercessory prayer, and healing prayer.

Don Perini has been influenced by the Charismatic Movement. He was baptised in the Spirit many years ago and received the gift of tongues. The Parish Cells stress the role of the Holy Spirit and refer to the need for baptism in the Spirit in the *Leaders Manual*.[20] The Cells see themselves as existing to evangelise, firstly their own members. When groups grow to have fourteen members they automatically split into two groups. They also

18. *Cell Leaders Training Manual: Parish Cell System Of Evangelization* (Milano: Parroccia St Eustorgio, 2006).
19. *Evangelii Nuntiandi*, par. 14.
20. Op. cit., 31.

feel called to evangelise people in society. For instance, members of the St Eustorgio cells go in twos into the busy streets of central Milan and talk to people who are out for the evening, taking drugs, or who are homeless. They sometimes invite them to come to the parish church where the Eucharist is exposed. Surprisingly, many people accept the invitation. When it seems appropriate they pray with their visitors or for them, sometimes in charismatic ways. While the training manual does not say anything explicit about the connection between charisms and evangelisation, that dimension is not totally absent. At the end of each cell meeting a designated amount of time is devoted to prayer for healing.

While Alpha seems to have been influenced by the third wave of renewal, the Parish Cells do not. However, they have been influenced, to a certain extent, by the second wave and accept that there is an interconnection between the power of the Holy Spirit, effective evangelisation, and some charismatic activity.

c) Harversters

Harvesters is a Catholic men's network in Britain. It has an informative website.[21] It has evolved within the Charismatic Movement in Britain. Only one of its many activities will be highlighted here. Each year the Harvesters organise three retreats which are attended by relatively large numbers of men. In 2006 there were 200 at one of them. A collection is made at each retreat in order to finance three men from the network of groups to go to Africa to offer material help and to evangelise. Early in 2005, for instance, the missionaries headed off to Tanzania with £30,000 to distribute to good causes. When they got to Dar es Salaam they conducted a Catholic miracle rally. One of the men, Roy Hendy, wrote in *Goodnews* magazine: 'The team fasted for two days in preparation for the ministry at the event. Gerard Pomfret, who is better known for running the bookstalls at charismatic conferences, had never ministered to such a huge group before, and found himself leading a healing service for 1400 people. As there were only three in the English team, and

---

21. http://www.harvesters.org.uk (accessed May 1st 2008)

because of the amount of people to be prayed for, the stretcher bearers were co-opted to help out and were prayed with to receive an anointing so that they could pray for people in the crowd as well. It was an amazing time. I have never seen so many healings and deliverances in my life, as at the Miracle Rally. One young woman had been bent up double all her life, and after a few minutes of prayer she straightened up before my eyes. She couldn't believe it. You couldn't doubt that the power of the Spirit was there. It certainly wasn't us. At one point I simply held up my crucifix and people around me fell down on the floor manifesting.'[22]

When Gerard Pomfret, a member of the trio, told his story at a summer retreat, it was one of the most moving and soul stirring things the men had ever heard. Gerard recounted how he had never led a miracle service before this. When he saw all the people, many of them with pressing needs, he wept profusely. Although he felt great compassion for them he felt powerless to do anything to alleviate their afflictions. Then he described how the Spirit of God came upon him in his weakness and infused him with the faith conviction that, with God's help, he would be able to minister effectively. By the grace of God hundreds of healings and deliverances occurred during the Miracle Rally. To hear Gerard's account was like listening to an account of how the Acts of the Apostles had come alive in the modern world.

BENEFITS OF THE CHARISMATIC APPROACH TO EVANGELISATION

Arguably, these are three of the benefits to the charismatic approach to evangelisation just described.

1) Pointers to the Supernatural
We live at a time when secularisation is widespread. Growing numbers of people, including many Catholics, are influenced by contemporary reductionist thinking and are skeptical about the supernatural. Lutheran theologian Langdon Gilkey drew attention to this phenomenon in the Post Vatican Two church in his *Catholicism Confronts Modernity: A Protestant View*.[23] Unbelievers

---

22. (Jan/Feb 2006), 33.
23. (New York: Seabury Press, 1975).

deny the existence of God, good and evil spirits, healings, miracles and the like. Liberal Christians, including some members of the clergy, accept the existence of God and an afterlife, but are doubtful about the reality of many supernatural entities and events. So whenever evangelisation is accompanied by deeds of power, they not only manifest the glory of God, they also manifest in a credible, experiential way the presence of the Beyond in the midst of everyday life. For instance, well-known Pentecostal leader, David Du Plessis has recounted in his book *Simple and Profound*, how he was once asked by a disciple of Rudolf Bultmann, 'What is your approach to the Bible?' 'To demythologise it,' he replied. Surprised by this answer, the questioner asked, 'How do you do this?' 'It is very simple,' Du Plessis responded, 'we Pentecostals take the things in the Bible that you say are myths, and we make them happen today so that they are demythologised!'[24]

2) Signs, Wonders, and Christian Apologetics

It is incumbent upon those who believe in the possibility of deeds of power, that they do two things. Firstly, they need to be careful not to make careless or exaggerated claims about supposed healings and miracles. For example, if people seem to be pain free as a result of prayer, it may be due to psycho-somatic causes because opiates can be released in the brains of those who trust in the healer as an authority figure.[25] In such cases the pain will return in a relatively short time. It is important to verify healings or miracles in a scientific way so that they will have greater credibility for people who are skeptical. Secondly, Christian apologists need to read the findings of modern science, especially quantum physics, in order to argue that we no longer live in the closed universe described by Newton which is ruled by the inexorable laws of efficient causality. Writers like Keith Ward,[26] John Polkingthorne,[27] Francis Collins[28] and others have

24. (Orleans, Mass.: Paraclete Press, 1986), 54.
25. See Robert Eagle, *A Guide to Alternative Medicine* (London: BBC, 1980).
26. *Divine Action: Examining God's Role in an Open and Emergent Universe* (West Conshohocken, PA.: Templeton Foundation Press, 2007).
27. *Faith, Science and Understanding* (New Haven: Yale University Press, 2001).
28. *The Language of God: A Scientist Presents Evidence for Belief* (New York: Free Press, 2006).

shown how we live in an open universe where belief in miracles does not necessarily require a *deus ex machina* intervention.[29] Charismatic manifestations support this contention.

3) The gifts of the Spirit and Ecumenism

Happily the Spirit and his gifts have been poured out in all denominations. Through their common exercise, Christians are being drawn closer to Jesus and therefore closer to one another. In an article entitled, 'Ecumenical Origins of the Charismatic Renewal,' Peter Hocken showed clearly that renewal in the Spirit and reconciliation have been virtually synonymous in the Charismatic Renewal.[30] Charisms, as Christians in Northern Ireland and elsewhere recognise, have a unique ability to build bridges of unity.

For example, a Catholic woman in Northern Ireland recently told me that she was doing some shopping in a Protestant area. In one store, she happened to get into conversation with a fellow customer who told her that she was suffering from a painful physical problem. The Catholic woman was touched by what the afflicted woman had shared with her. She asked if she would like to prayed with. The woman answered yes, so they went to a quiet, secluded part of the shop. As the Catholic woman prayed for her Protestant acquaintance she had a strong sense of God's love for her, and the Lord's desire, then and there, to help her by means of his healing power. The prayer lasted for only a few minutes, but it was full of care and conviction. Then the women parted, and returned to their respective homes.

A few days later the Protestant woman returned to the shop. She was looking for information about the person who had prayed for her, because in the interim she had been completely healed. She described what the mysterious stranger looked like. The shopkeeper told her, to her complete surprise, that she was a Catholic woman, from a nearby town. Later, he contacted his Catholic customer to tell her the good news. Not surprisingly, when a Christian with expectant faith performs a deed of power for a member of another church, not only does it manifest the

---

29. See Pat Collins CM, 'Towards a Theology of Prayer of Petition,' *Milltown Studies* (Winter 2000), 1-14.
30. *Goodnews* (Silver jubilee of Charismatic Renewal edition 1992), 51-53.

presence and power of God's kingdom, it also tends to break down the dividing wall of division that sometimes separates Catholics from Protestants and *vice versa*. In other words it is a powerful means of reconciliation.

CONCLUSION

One could question some of the theology informing the different approaches to evangelisation which have been described in this chapter. However, it would be true to say that they all stress the importance of Holy Spirit and all of them are open, to a greater or lesser extent, to the possibility that the truth of the gospel proclamation, which is rooted in inspired revelation, may be demonstrated by deeds of power such as healing, exorcism, and miracle working. Peter Wagner had a good deal of impressive statistical evidence in mind when he wrote,[31] 'I am proud to be among those who are advocating power evangelism as an important tool for the fulfilling of the great commission in our day. One of the reasons that I am so enthusiastic is that it is working. Across the board, the most effective evangelism in today's world is accompanied by manifestations of supernatural power.'[32]

31. David B. Barrett, George T. Kurian, and Todd M. Johnson, eds. *World Christian Encyclopedia* (New York: Oxford University Press USA, 2001).
32. *The Third Wave of the Holy Spirit: Encountering the Power of Signs and Wonders Today* (Ann Arbor: Vine Books, 1988), 87.

CHAPTER EIGHT

You will be my Witnesses

Those of us who feel called to be Christ's witnesses (cf Acts 1:8) face a difficult task. In the Western world in general, and in Europe in particular, we have seen the silent defection of many millions of people. For the first time in history, we live in an era when God seems to have little or no role in the lives of a growing number of people. Some are avowed atheists, many others are practical or anonymous atheists.[1] Because of the notion of the closed universe, which can be traced back to Isaac Newton, educated people, including liberal Christians, are skeptical about the existence of a supernatural realm. As a result, they assume, *a priori,* that neither God nor angels can have any discernable influence in the world. If the human condition is going to be improved, it can only happen as a result of the application of human intelligence and effort, e.g. in the medical field.

In Western culture, evangelisation is not a matter of telling people who never believed in God about Jesus Christ. Rather they have to convey the good news to people who have already tried Christianity and rejected it, at least at the notional level of experience. However, it is arguable, as Karl Rahner once suggested when talking about the controversial notion of 'anonymous Christians,' that unthematic openness to God and justifying grace are active in the lives of many people beyond the pale of Christianity.[2] It could be argued that Pope Paul VI had something akin to this point in mind when he wrote in *EN* par. 55, 'In this ... modern world ... and this is a paradox, one cannot deny

---

1. Jacques Maritain, 'The Meaning of Contemporary Atheism', *A Maritain Reader,* ed. & trs, Donald and Idella Gallagher (New York: Image Books, 1966), 107-108. He says, 'Practical atheists believe that they believe in God but in actual fact they deny his existence by their deeds and the testimony of their behaviour.'
2. There is a good summary in Patrick Burke, *Reinterpreting Rahner: A Critical Study of his Major Themes* (New York: Fordham University Press, 2002), 174-176.

the existence of real steppingstones to Christianity, and of evangelical values at least in the form of a sense of emptiness or nostalgia. It would not be an exaggeration to say that there exists a powerful and tragic appeal to be evangelised.'

In some ways the observations of Rahner and the Pope are borne out by empirical evidence. For instance, in an article entitled, 'Is Britain's Soul Waking-Up?'[3] David Hay and Kate Hunt have referred to results of interesting research conducted in the UK. While it confirmed that fewer people go to church than ever before, paradoxically there has been a dramatic rise in the numbers claiming to have had religious experience. Over the past 25 years there has been a startling 110% rise in the number of men and women reporting a sense of a mysterious Power or Presence, beyond their everyday selves. Hay and Hunt remark: 'We are in the midst of an explosive spiritual upsurge.' They go on to say: 'We know, from the research we have done, that most people's spirituality is a long way away from institutional religion. This spirituality has little doctrinal content, and few people have more than the vaguest remnants of religious language to express their experience of God. The phrase we commonly hear is "I definitely believe in Something; there's Something there." Their spirituality is based upon a longing for meaning.' Hay has commented elsewhere that what characterises spiritual pilgrims in Britain is that they are in 'quest mode,' in sociologist Daniel Batson's sense.[4] In contrast to Gordon Allport who talked in the 1950s about extrinsic and intrinsic religion, Batson said there was an intermediate group of spiritual pilgrims who had more questions than answers.

No wonder a new evangelisation is needed to name and build upon that subliminal awareness. It is not all that surprising that God has once again granted the charisms to a growing number of believers. It seems that the main reason for this Pentecostal blessing is the ability of the supernatural gifts to bear witness to the power and presence of God in a secular world. It is significant that in 1 Cor 12:7 Paul describes the

---

3. *The Tablet* (24 June 2000).
4. 'The Spirituality of Adults in Britain – Some Recent Research,' *Scottish Journal of Healthcare Chaplaincy*, vol 5, no 1, (2002). http://www.sach.org.uk/journal/0501p04_hay. pdf (accessed Oct 7th 2008).

charisms as manifestations. They are inspired words and actions, epiphanies of a charismatic kind, which make the Spirit of God to be tangible and known, in such a way as to invite, and evoke faith. At this stage we will look at a number of points that will be relevant in the new evangelisation.

GOOD NEWS TO THE POOR

As was noted in the second chapter, Luke 4:18-21 informs us that when Jesus preached for the first time in his local synagogue, he firstly read the text: 'The Spirit of the Lord is on me, because he has anointed me to preach good news to the poor. He has sent me to proclaim freedom for the prisoners and recovery of sight for the blind, to release the oppressed, to proclaim the year of the Lord's favour.' This text is very important because it is the mission statement of Jesus. He was declaring what he was about, namely bringing the good news of the coming of the kingdom to the poor. Although it is a controversial point, it is arguable that the gospel can only be received by the poor. Who are they? For many years there has been a lot of debate about this issue. Much of it has generated more heat than light. However, in biblical terms the poor can either be the materially poor, or the poor in spirit. That distinction is clear in Luke's and Matthew's versions of the beatitudes. In Lk 6:20 Jesus declared, 'Blessed are you who are poor, for yours is the kingdom of God,' and in Mt 5:3-4 he said, 'Blessed are the poor in spirit, for theirs is the kingdom of heaven.'

The poor are those who, for material or other reasons, experience 'creature feeling,' to use Rudolf Otto's phrase, and are consciously aware of their need for God. In modern times Blessed Teresa of Calcutta had a good grasp of the fact that, whereas in developing countries people were more likely to acknowledge their need of God as a result of material need, in the developed countries of the West, people are more likely to acknowledge that need as a result of experiencing psycho-spiritual problems such as loneliness, addiction, depression, anxiety etc. Blessed Teresa used to refer to them as the new poor. In developed nations, the needs of the 'new poor' are hard to meet. Their problems, says Mother Teresa, 'are deep down, at the bottom of their hearts ... here you have a different kind of poverty – a poverty of the spirit, of loneliness, and being unwanted. And that is the worst disease in the world today, not tuberculosis or leprosy.'[5] Many people share activities and tasks, but not themselves. Therefore, it would probably be true to say that in individualistic cultures such as ours, compassionate love is the greatest need. As Mother Teresa puts it: 'People today are hungry for love, for understanding love, which is much greater and which is the only answer to loneliness and great poverty.'[6]

I teach the psychology of religion in a third level college. I have sometimes been surprised by the way in which psychologists confirm Bl Teresa's observation. For example, Viktor Frankl says that many people who do not have a sense of unconditional meaning in life can suffer from an existential vacuum and existential frustration. He wrote: 'This existential vacuum, along with other causes, can result in neurotic illness.'[7] Frankl also believed that when people suppressed their religious sense, their unfulfilled desire for meaning would be displaced into unhealthy attitudes and behaviours. They would end up making things like possessions, pleasure, power, and position into idolatrous substitutes for uncreated meaning.

Frankl believed that common problems in Western countries, such as depression, aggression and addiction were often rooted in the experience of existential frustration. He explained: 'Sometimes the frustrated will to meaning is vicariously compensated for by a will to power, including the most primitive form of the will to power, the will to money. In other cases the place of the frustrated will to meaning is taken by the will to pleasure. That is why existential frustration often leads to sexual compensation. We can observe in such cases that the sexual libido becomes rampant in the existential vacuum.'[8] It is interesting to note that shortly before his death, Pope John Paul II seemed to echo Frankl's evaluation when he wrote in *The Church in Europe*, 'Among the troubling indications of the loss of a

---

5. *Mother Teresa of Calcutta, A Gift for God* (London: Fount, 1981), 76.
6. Desmond Doig, *Mother Teresa: Her People and her Work*, (London: Fount, 1978), 139.
7. *Psychotherapy and Existentialism* (London: Pelican Book, 1967), 51.
8. *Man's Search For Meaning* (New York: Washington Square Press, 1985), 129-130.

Christian memory are the inner emptiness that grips many people and the loss of meaning in life. The signs and fruits of this existential anguish include, in particular, the diminishing number of births, the decline in the number of vocations to the priesthood and religious life, and the difficulty, if not the outright refusal, to make lifelong commitments, including marriage. We find ourselves before a widespread existential fragmentation. A feeling of loneliness is prevalent; divisions and conflicts are on the rise.'[9]

Jesus satisfied material and psycho-spiritual needs in a charismatic way when he was evangelising. For instance, when people were hungry he multiplied the loaves and fish (Mt 14:16-21); when they were oppressed by evil spirits he delivered them (Mk 5:1-13); when they felt that they were under a curse with no hope of salvation he assured them that they were blessed and that the kingdom of God would be theirs. To be effective evangelisers of the poor, the evangelists themselves need to be people who are in real solidarity with the people they wish to evangelise as a result of sharing in their experience of poverty in one way or another. A person who has acknowledged his or her own poverty, and has found that Jesus fed him or her with the manna of God's saving word and grace, is equipped as one beggar to tell other beggars where to find the bread of life. Many evangelists know from personal experience that it is those who humbly acknowledge their poverty who are more likely to have firm faith in God, and God's power to act even to the point of healings and miracles. The story about the men from Harvesters, and their effective ministry in Tanzania, seems to illustrate that point.

INSPIRED PREACHING

It is a striking fact that Jesus said that he was anointed by the Spirit in order to proclaim the coming of the kingdom of God. What is surprising is the fact that he denied any originality. He testified: 'I do nothing on my own but speak just what the Father has taught me' (Jn 8:28), and 'whatever I say is just what the Father has told me to say' (Jn 12:50). As the Word made flesh

---

9. Par. 8.

Jesus enjoyed perfect union with his Father. As he said, 'I and the Father are one' (Jn 10:30). Nevertheless, although the word of God welled within him, he acknowledged that it had its origin in God the Father. Like Jesus, the preachers and teachers of the Christian community should only proclaim what has been revealed to them in prayer. Speaking to a younger colleague, who had been appointed superior of a seminary in 1656, St Vincent de Paul, founder of the Congregation of the Mission, said, 'An important point, and one to which you should carefully devote yourself, is to establish a close union between yourself and the Lord in prayer ... When in doubt, have recourse to God and say to him: "O Lord, you are the Father of light, teach me what I ought to do in this circumstance." I give you this advice not only for those difficulties which will cause you anxiety, but also *that you may learn from God directly what you shall have to teach* [my italics], following the example of Moses who proclaimed to the people of Israel only that which God had inspired him to say.'[10]

To do what Vincent advocates, preachers and teachers need to bring their poverty to God by engaging in regular periods of scripture prayer of a contemplative kind. In his *Summa Theologica* St Thomas Aquinas wrote, 'The object of faith is not the statement, but the reality.'[11] Many of us are people whose lives are centred on the spoken and written word. We are familiar with many things that scripture and tradition have to say about God. However, we often feel imprisoned by the words and unable to sense and experience the realities that they signify. But there can be inspirational periods in prayer when, by the grace of God, we break through to the realities that the words of scripture signify. The word of God as a noun upon the page, which is objectively true in itself, becomes a living noun that leaps from the page, alive with subjective meaning and relevance, into the depths of the heart. There it reveals the presence and purposes of God.

Needless to say, the praying person needs to engage in discernment of spirits in order to ascertain whether the inspirations

---

10. Quoted by Andre Dodin, *Vincent de Paul and Charity* (New York: New City Press, 1993), 82.
11. ST I-II, q. 1, a. 2, ad 2

or revelations he or she has received are truly from God or not. There are many helpful books on this subject such as Jules Toner's excellent *Discerning God's Will: Ignatius of Loyola's Teaching on Christian Decision Making*[12] and Chris Aridas's *Discernment: Seeking God in Every Situation*.[13] Secondly, while being careful to avoid illuminism, would-be evangelists have to teach and preach those things the Lord has taught them as a result of their prayerful reflection. Thirdly, the truth of what is proclaimed needs to demonstrated by means of the witness of a holy life, spiritual and corporal works of mercy, such as those listed by the church,[14] action for justice which is an integral aspect of evangelisation,[15] and if God so wills it, by means of charismatic activity, especially deeds of power such as healings and exorcism.

LET THE DEED BE ADDED TO THE WORD

Commenting on the first line of the Creed, 'I believe in God,' par. 156 of the *CCC* says: 'What moves us to believe is not the fact that revealed truths appear as true and intelligible in the light of our natural reason: we believe because of the authority of God himself who reveals them, who can neither deceive nor be deceived.' So 'that the submission of our faith might nevertheless be in accordance with reason, God willed that external proofs of his revelation should be joined to the internal helps of the Holy Spirit.' Thus the miracles of Christ and the saints, prophecies, the church's growth and holiness, and her fruitfulness and stability 'are the most certain signs of divine revelation,

---

12. (St Louis: The Institute of Jesuit Sources, 1991).
13. (New Jersey: Resurrection Press, 2004)
14. Par. 2247 of the *Catechism of the Catholic Church* says: 'The works of mercy are: Instructing, advising, consoling, comforting are spiritual works of mercy, as are forgiving and bearing wrongs patiently. The corporal works of mercy are: feeding the hungry, sheltering the homeless, clothing the naked, visiting the sick and imprisoned, burying the dead and giving alms to the poor.' They are mostly derived from Mt 25:31-46.
15. The Synod of Bishops of 1971, said in *Justice in the World*, 'Action on behalf of justice and the transformation of society is integral to the mission of the church and the preaching of the gospel, or, in other words, of the church's mission for the redemption of the human race and its liberation from every oppressive situation.'

adapted to the intelligence of all;' they are 'motives of credibility' (*motiva credibilitatis*), which show that the assent of faith is 'by no means a blind impulse of the mind.' This important assertion situates the working of deeds of power within the context of faith in divine revelation. As was also noted in chapter two, Jesus asked those who heard him speak to believe what he said on the basis of the authenticating deeds of supernatural power that he performed. He declared: 'If I am not doing the works of my Father, then do not believe me. But if I do them, even though you do not believe me, believe the works, so that you may know and understand that the Father is in me and I am in the Father' (Jn 10:37-38).[16]

There was a saying which was attributed to Hanina Ben Dosa, a contemporary of Jesus: 'He whose actions exceed his wisdom, his wisdom shall endure, but he whose wisdom exceeds his actions, his wisdom shall not endure.'[17] Not surprisingly, the apostles said similar things. In the letters attributed to St Paul, there are a number of texts which bear this out. For instance he said: 'Our gospel came to you not simply with words, but also with power, with the Holy Spirit and with deep conviction' (1 Thess 1:5). On another occasion he testified: 'My message and my preaching were not with wise and persuasive words, but with a demonstration of the Spirit's power' (1 Cor 2:41). In many ways Heb 2:3-4 summed up the Pauline attitude: 'This salvation which was first announced by the Lord, was confirmed to us by those who heard him. God also testified to it by signs, wonders and various miracles, and gifts of the Holy Spirit distributed according to his will.' Chapter three noted how St Thomas rejected the cessationist argument and fully endorsed the Pauline point of view. Implicit in this perspective is a kind of economy of evangelisation. The example of the miracle service conducted by the Harvesters in Tanzania indicates that God seems to perform deeds of power, mainly for the sake of the poor and unbelievers.[18] In an age like our own, where there is

---

16. Cf Paul VI, 'With Evangelical Signs,' (par. 12), *Evangelii Nuntiandi*.

17. Quoted by Gerald Sloyan, *Jesus in Focus* (Mystic: Twenty Third Publications, 1983), 35-41.

18. It is clear from the gospels that Jesus was motivated to perform deeds of power, primarily by compassion (Cf., Mt 20:34; Lk 7:13). Arguably, deeds of power can be performed among believers, primarily

such widespread unbelief, there is a great need for the demonstration of the Spirit to accompany the proclamation of the word.

The subject of simple and solemn exorcism is also an important topic. It was noted in chapter two that it is debatable whether exorcism is a charism, a gift *gratis datae* or not. However, there is no doubt that it is not only needed occasionally, it can bear powerful witness to the liberating power of the risen Lord. Jesus was an exorcist and commissioned the apostles to exorcise in his name as an integral aspect of evangelisation (Mk 16:17). The contemporary church teaches that the devil exists. For instance, in 1975 the Congregation for the Doctrine of the Faith published a document entitled, *Christian Faith and Demonology*. It stated: 'We repeat ... that though still emphasising in our day the real existence of the demonic, the church has no intention ... of proposing an alternative explanation which would be more acceptable to reason. Its desire is simply to remain faithful to the gospel and its requirements.' On 30 June 1972, Pope Paul VI said that he sensed 'that from somewhere or other, the smoke of Satan has entered the temple of God.'[19] Not surprisingly he said a few months later on 15 November 1972, 'What are the church's greatest needs at the present time? Don't be surprised at our answer and don't write it off as simplistic or even superstitious: one of the church's greatest needs is to be defended against the evil we call the Devil.'[20] In 1999 a new rite of exorcism replaced the one that had been used ever since 1614 AD. Finally, canon 1172 of the 1986 *Code of Canon Law* states that only a priest appointed by the bishop can perform a solemn, as opposed to a simple exorcism. In spite of all these facts many bishops have failed to appoint an official exorcist in their dioceses. In Ireland for example, not one official exorcist has been appointed in living

---

as expressions of divine compassion rather than as demonstrations of the truth of the gospel proclamation.

19. http://www.vatican.va/holy_father/paul_vi/homilies/1972/documents/hf_p-vi_hom_19720629_it.html (accessed May 9th 2008).

20. http://www.papalencyclicals./Paul06/p6devil.htm (accessed May 9th 2008).

memory. But there are signs of hope. On 27 December 2007 Fr Gabriele Amorth, the chief exorcist of Rome, said in an interview: 'Thanks be to God that we have a Pope who has decided to fight the Devil head on. Now bishops are to be obliged to have a number of established exorcists for their diocese. Too many bishops are not taking this seriously and are not delegating priests to fight against the Devil – you have to hunt high and low for a proper trained exorcist. Thankfully Pope Benedict XVI believes in the existence and danger of evil – from the time he was in charge of the Congregation for the Doctrine of the Faith.'

Early in 2005, the Legionaries of Christ initiated a course on exorcism in their Regina Apostolorum University, in Rome. There is a pastoral need for concerned priests and laity, together with help from sympathetic experts from the medical profession, to equip themselves for this difficult ministry. A few very helpful handbooks on the subject are available.[21] I am convinced on the basis of some personal experience,[22] that effective deliverance from evil spirits through the power of God, manifests the presence and liberating power of the risen Lord in a uniquely powerful and effective way in secularised societies.

A PARADIGMATIC EXPERIENCE

A number of years ago, I belonged to a large prayer group. At one point, sixteen of the more experienced members decided to form an auxiliary community group which met on a different night. At the inaugural gathering I gave a keynote address which suggested that we should aim to live like the early Christians as depicted in Acts 4:32-36. Through the power of the Holy Spirit they had realised the ancient Greek ideal of friendship by being conformed to the mind and heart of Christ while having all things in common. When I asked for reactions, I was disappointed to find that many of those present thought that this ideal was far too demanding. Happily, however, one of the chief objectors got a word of knowledge. He said, that if we read

21. Cf Francis Mc Nutt, *Deliverance From Evil Spirits: A Manual* (London: Hodder & Stoughton, 1996); Neal Lozano, *Unbound: A Practical Guide to Deliverance* (Grand Rapids, MI.: Chosen, 2007).
22. Pat Collins CM, 'The Paranormal and Spirituality', *Mind and Spirit* (Dublin: Columba, 2006), 113-128.

Sir 6:14-18, we would get God's perspective on the issue. I quickly found the passage. It was about friendship in the Lord!

Some time later, during a memorable meeting, one member of the community group read Lk 6:36-39, 'Be merciful, just as your Father is merciful. Do not judge, and you will not be judged. Do not condemn, and you will not be condemned. Forgive, and you will be forgiven. Give, and it will be given to you. A good measure, pressed down, shaken together and run-ning over, will be poured into your lap. For with the measure you use, it will be measured to you.' She shared how this pas-sage, about unconditional mercy, had inspired her. Then she spontaneously knelt on the floor and said: 'I promise to refrain from criticising, judging or condemning anyone in this group, either in thought or word. If I break this promise, I will publicly confess my fault and seek forgiveness.' There was a stunned si-lence. Then, one by one, everyone present, freely knelt down and made the same promise. That Spirit-prompted agreement had remarkable effects. Jesus has assured us that, 'whatever measure you use in giving – large or small – it will be used to measure what is given back to you' (Lk 6:38). Justifying grace, as we well know, is not the fruit of good works. Although this un-merited gift of God is always freely available to us, we only ex-perience its liberating power in so far as we put aside the scales of justice, by refraining from judging, condemning or resenting other people while offering them the undeserved gift of our merciful love. Like a sanctuary lamp within, members of the community group continued to be consciously aware of God's saving grace as long as we maintained a merciful attitude. As time passed we found that our trust levels grew greatly. As a re-sult, we felt more closely united than ever before. We were no longer afraid that anyone would talk or think in a critical way about us, behind our backs. Our community group became a place of psychological safety where each person could blossom, by being his or her own true self. While we had always been committed to praising the Lord, as we became more united, there was more joy. A new gift of enthusiastic praise was re-leased, one which was both loud and long. One of our favourite scriptural passage was Sir 43:31-34 which encourages people to redouble their praises, because God is more than worthy of all the appreciation we can express. Although we had often desired the gifts of the Spirit, only a few of them had been granted to us. But when we made love our aim by agreeing to fast from criticism and to praise God with conviction, all the gifts described in 1 Cor 12:8-10 were poured out on different members of the group, including the gifts of prophecy and healing.

I can remember that during that wonderful time of growth we had a desire to evangelise together. We prayed that some parish priest would invite us to his parish to conduct a mission. From a human point of view it was unlikely to happen. But in answer to our prayers the Lord intervened in a providential way. One evening a couple came to our prayer meeting with their baby who had a hole in the heart. She had been scheduled for surgery. Besides the parents, I was the only one in the prayer meeting who knew about this serious health problem. When I looked at the child I could see that its lips were an unhealthy blue colour. At one point during the meeting one of our regular members got a word of knowledge. He said that he could see a heart in his mind's eye. It had a hole in it! I revealed that in actual fact there was a baby in the room who was suffering from that very complaint. I encouraged everyone present to pray with great faith and love. A few days later the baby was brought to hospital for a preliminary checkup prior to the planned operation. The doctors were non-plussed because they found that there was no hole in the girl's heart. Word of this healing spread in the parish where the family lived. The parish priest was so impressed that he sent the prayer group an invitation to visit his parish in order to conduct a short mission. Our prayers had been answered.

The day before the mission was due to take place I was feeling anxious and prayed fervently for divine guidance. To cut a longer story short I was led by a word of knowledge to look at a designated page in a particular volume of the *New Catholic Encyclopedia*. When I opened it I was disappointed at first. It contained a black and white photograph of an ancient parchment with contained some writing in a foreign language. I asked a learned colleague if he knew what it was about. He said, yes, it was a Hebrew version of Josh 1:6-7. I ran to my room, opened my Bible at the appropriate place and read: 'Be strong and courageous, because you will lead these people to inherit the land ... Be strong and very courageous ... do not turn from it to the right or to the left, that you may be successful wherever you go.' Fortified by this assurance, I arrived in the parish and gathered the team in the church sacristy to pray, and to assign each person his or her task. I asked if anyone had got any guidance from the Lord. One man answered, 'Yes, last night I was led to Josh 1:6-7.' When I explained that I had been led to the very same verses we were much encouraged, feeling that God was truly with us as in all we were hoping to do. Some time later we had a penance service which was followed by a Mass for healing. We removed the front benches so there would be room for wheelchairs and stretchers. The church was filled for the ceremony, and by the grace of God a number of people experienced either physical or emotional healing as a result of receiving the anointing of the sick and being prayed with by members of our mission team. The whole event was like a page from the Acts of the Apostles coming alive. We had been led to the parish by God; we were encouraged by God; we proclaimed God's word; and God confirmed what was said by the deeds of power he performed. For me, and the others, it was an example of how the gifts of the Spirit can make effective evangelisation possible. To this day, that mission and the many events that led up to it have become my evangelistic template or paradigm. It would probably be true to say that the idea of this book was first prompted by that experience.

CONCLUSION

In view of all that has been said in this book, it is not really surprising to find that, speaking to an International Conference, 19 May 1975, Pope Paul VI said: 'How could this "spiritual renewal" not be a chance for the church and the world?'[23] Some time later, Pope John Paul II echoed those sentiments when he addressed a group of international leaders of the Charismatic Renewal on 11 December 1979. He said: 'I am convinced that this movement is a very important component of the entire re-

---

23. Kilian McDonnell, *Open the Windows – The Popes and Charismatic Renewal* (South Bend, Ind.: Greenlawn, 1989), 13.

newal of the Church.'[24] We conclude with some words that were spoken by Pope Paul VI when he departed from his prepared text and spontaneously said at the launch of Cardinal Suenens's book *A New Pentecost?* 'How wonderful it would be if the Lord would again pour out the charisms in increased abundance, in order to make the church fruitful, beautiful and marvellous, and to enable it to win the attention and astonishment of the profane and secularised world.'[25]

> Spirit, dispenser of charisms to everyone;
> Spirit of wisdom and knowledge, who so loves us all,
> You fill the prophets, perfect the apostles,
> Strengthen the martyrs, inspire the teachers with teaching!
> To you, our Paraclete God,
> We send up our supplications along with this fragrant incense.
> We ask you to renew us with your holy gifts,
> To come down upon us as you came down on the apostles in the upper room.
> Pour out your charisms upon us,
> Fill us with knowledge of your teaching;
> Make us temples of your glory,
> Let us be overcome by the wine of your grace.
> Grant that we may live for you, be of one mind with you, and adore you,
> You the pure, you the holy, God Spirit Paraclete.[26]
> *(Office of Pentecost used in the Syriac Rite)*

---

24. Ibid., 26. The Holy Father said in that same address, that ever since childhood he had said a daily prayer to the Holy Spirit that his father had recommended. As a result, he stated, 'I have always belonged to this renewal in the Holy Spirit ... I can understand all the different charisms. All of them are part of the riches of the Lord.'
25. Edward O Connor, *Pope Paul and the Spirit*, op. cit, 212.
26. *Pontificale Syrorum*, in E.-P. Siman, *L'experience de l'Espirit* (Paris: Beauchesne, 1971), 309.

Bibliography

Addison, Doug. *Prophecy, Dreams, and Evangelism: Revealing God's Love Through Divine Encounters*. North Sutton, New Hampshire: Streams Publishing House, 2005.

Ashley, O.P., Benedict M. Thomas Aquinas. *The Gifts of the Spirit. Selected Spiritual Writings*. New York: New City Press, 1995.

Bittlinger, James Arthur. *Gifts and Graces: Commentary in 1 Corinthians 12-14*. New Ed. edition. London: Hodder & Stoughton, 1973.

— *Gifts and Ministries*. Grand Rapids: Eerdmans, 1973.

Burgess, Stanley M., Maas, Eduard van der, eds. *The New International Dictionary of the Pentecostal and Charismatic Movements*. Grand Rapids, Mi.: Zondervan, 2002.

Cantalamessa, Raniero. *The Holy Spirit in the Life of Jesus: The Mystery of Christ's Baptism*. Collegeville, Minnesota: The Liturgical Press, 1994.

— *Come Holy Spirit: Meditations on the Veni Creator*. Collegeville, Minnesota: The Liturgical Press, 2003.

Carson, D. A. *Showing the Spirit: A Theological Exposition of 1 Corinthians 12-14*. Grand Rapids: Baker Book House, 1987.

Congar, Yves. *I Believe in the Holy Spirit (Milestones in Catholic Theology)* New Edition. New York: Herder & Herder, 1997.

Cordes, Paul Joseph. *Charisms and the New Evangelisation*. Middlegreen, Slough: St Paul Publications, 1992.

Cox, Harvey. *Fire from Heaven: The Rise of Pentecostal Spirituality and the Reshaping of Religion in the Twenty-first Century*. New York: Addison-Wesley, 1995.

de Lambertinis, Prosperi Cardinalis. *De Servorum Dei Beatificatione, et Beatorum Canonizatione*, vol 4. Roma: Prati, Mdcccxxxxi.

Dulles, S.J., Avery, 'The Charism of the New Evangelizer,' *Retrieving Charisms for the Twenty-First Century*, ed. Doris Donnelly. Collegeville: The Liturgical Press, 1999.

Dunn, James D. G. *Jesus and the Spirit: A Study of the Religious and Charismatic Experience of Jesus and the First Christians as Reflected in the New Testament*. Philadelphia: Westminster, 1975.

du Plessis, David. *Simple and Profound*. Orleans, Mass: Paraclete Press, 1986.

Fee, Gordon D., ed. *The New International Commentary on the New Testament.* Vol 6, *The First Epistle to the Corinthians*, by Gordon D. Fee. Grand Rapids, Michigan: Eerdmans, 1987.

— *God's Empowering Presence: The Holy Spirit in the Letters of Paul.* Peabody, Mass.: Hendrickson, 1994.

Green, Michael. *Evangelism in the Early Church.* London: Hodder & Stoughton, 1970.

— *I Believe in the Holy Spirit.* Grand Rapids: Eerdmans, 1975.

Harrington, Daniel J., S.J., ed. Sacra Pagina Series. Vol 7, *First Corinthians*, by Raymond F. Collins. Collegeville: The Liturgical Press, 1999.

Hocken, Peter. *The Glory and the Shame: Reflections on the 20th-Century Outpouring of the Holy Spirit.* Guildford: Eagle, 1994.

John of the Cross, St. *Ascent of Mount Carmel*, Book 3, chaps 30-32. Brewster, MA: Paraclete Press, 2002.

Lambertini, Prospero (Benedict XIV). *Treatise on the Beatification and Canonization of the Servants of God* (*Heroic Virtue*, Vol 3). New York: Edward Duignan & Brother, 1851.

Macchia, Frank D. *Baptized in the Spirit: A Global Pentecostal Theology.* Grand Rapids, Michigan: Zondervan, 2006.

McDonnell, Kilian and Montague, George T. *Christian Initiation and Baptism in the Holy Spirit: Evidence from the first Eight Centuries.* Collegeville: Liturgical Press, 1991.

Martin, Ralph and Williamson, Peter, eds. *John Paul II and the New Evangelization: How You can Bring the Good News to Others.* Cincinnati, Ohio: St Anthony Messenger Press, 2006.

Montague, George. *The Holy Spirit: Growth of a Biblical Tradition.* Eugene, Or.: Wipf & Stock Publishers, 2006.

— *The Spirit and his Gifts: The Biblical background of Spirit-baptism, Tongue-speaking, and Prophecy.* New York: Paulist Press, 1974.

— *Still Riding the Wind: Learning the Ways of the Spirit.* Ann Arbor: Word of Life, 1974.

Njiru, Paul Kariuki. *Charisms and the Holy Spirit's Activity in the Body of Christ: An Exegetical-Theological Study of 1 Corinthians 12:4-11 and Romans 12:6-8.* Testi Gregoriana Serie Theologia 86. Rome: Editrice Pontificia Universita Gregoriana, 2002.

Orr, William F. and Walther, James Arthur. *The Anchor Bible, 1 Corinthians: A New Translation, Introduction with a Study of the Life of*

Paul, Notes and Commentary. Garden City, New York: Doubleday & Company, Inc., 1976.

Sneck, William Joseph. *Charismatic Spiritual Gifts: A Phenomenological Analysis.* Washington, D.C.: University Press of America, Inc., 1981.

St Thomas Aquinas. *Commentary on the First Epistle to the Corinthians.* Trs Fabian Larcher, O.P. and Daniel Keating. Naples, Florida: Aquinas Center for Theological Renewal, 2006. http://www. aquinas.avemaria.edu/Aquinas-Corinthians.pdf. (accessed 4 April 2008)

— *Summa Contra Gentiles.* Annotated Translation (With some Abridgement) by Joseph Rickaby, S.J. London: Burns Oates, 1905. http://www.nd.edu/Departments/Maritain/etext/gc.htm. (accessed 4 April 2008)

— *Summa Theologiae.* Ages Software Version 1. Albany, Or: Books for the Ages, 1997.

— *Summa Theologica* in Three Volumes. Translated by Fathers of the English Dominican Province. New York: Benzinger Bros., Inc., 1947.

— *The Summa Theologiae: A Concise Translation.* Edited by Timothy Mc Dermott. London: Methuen, 1991.

Weddell, Sherry. *The Catholic Spiritual Gifts Inventory*, 3rd Edition. Colorado Springs: The Siena Institute Press, 1998.

Wagner, C. Peter. *The Third Wave of the Holy Spirit: Encountering the Power of Signs and Wonders Today.* Ann Arbor: Servant Publications Vine Books, 1988.

Wimber, John and Springer, Kevin. *Power Evangelism: Signs and Wonders Today,* 2nd Revised ed. London: Hodder & Stoughton Religious, 1997.

— *Power Healing.* London: Hodder & Stoughton, 1986.

— *A Brief Sketch of Signs and Wonders through the Church Age.* Placentia, California: Vineyard Christian Fellowship, 1984.

— *Signs and Wonders and Church Growth.* Placentia, California: Vineyard Ministries International, 1984.

Index